CHRISTIAN BASES OF WORLD ORDER

CHRISTIAN BASES OF WORLD ORDER

The Merrick Lectures for 1943

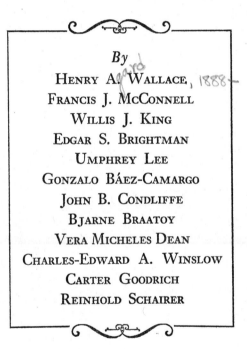

By

HENRY Agard WALLACE, 1888–

FRANCIS J. McCONNELL

WILLIS J. KING

EDGAR S. BRIGHTMAN

UMPHREY LEE

GONZALO BÁEZ-CAMARGO

JOHN B. CONDLIFFE

BJARNE BRAATOY

VERA MICHELES DEAN

CHARLES-EDWARD A. WINSLOW

CARTER GOODRICH

REINHOLD SCHAIRER

ABINGDON-COKESBURY PRESS

New York • Nashville

CHRISTIAN BASES OF WORLD ORDER
COPYRIGHT, MCMXLIII
BY WHITMORE & STONE

43 - 51138

SET UP, PRINTED, AND BOUND BY THE
PARTHENON PRESS AT NASHVILLE, TEN-
NESSEE, UNITED STATES OF AMERICA

FOREWORD

WHATEVER THE PARTICULAR FORM OF THE POLITICAL PEACE, the fundamental needs of men and society everywhere will still press for solution. A military victory will not solve these problems, although of course the major aspects of the peace are inevitably being determined by the conduct of the war. The military victory, however, will create the conditions under which free men can undertake to meet these human needs. World order has a moral and spiritual base, and the fundamental issues which are involved in world order are the concern of men of good will everywhere. World order is peculiarly related to the world mission of the Christian church.

The twelve chapters in this volume do not attempt any blueprint for the peace table or any detailed programs for either church or state. They do, however, lift into prominence certain Christian bases of world order and factors involved in it. These lectures, therefore, are vital and prophetic contributions to American thought in postwar planning.

The twelve chapters comprise the Merrick Lectures for 1943 of Ohio Wesleyan University, Delaware, Ohio. Upon the invitation of the University, the lectures were a part of the Conference on Christian Bases of World Order held at the University, March 8-12, 1943. Three hundred church leaders and representatives of the University constituted the Conference, which discussed the lectures and the findings of twelve study groups or seminars, one on each subject, organized in as many centers throughout the United States. Each chapter states the problem on the

5

topic assigned. The study groups attempted to answer the question, "What does this problem mean for the message and program of the church, especially in its overseas work?" The findings of the seminars, a summary of the discussions, the bibliography, and other material suitable for the increasing number of study groups on foreign policy and on the Christian world mission are to be published separately.

RALPH E. DIFFENDORFER

CONTENTS

THE INTRODUCTORY LECTURE

Practical Religion in the World of Tomorrow . .   9
    HENRY A. WALLACE

FUNDAMENTAL CHRISTIAN PRINCIPLES

God and the World We Live In 21
    FRANCIS J. McCONNELL

The Christian Conception of Man 45
    WILLIS J. KING

A Christian View of Nature 67
    EDGAR S. BRIGHTMAN

The Spiritual Basis of Democracy 85
    UMPHREY LEE

FACTORS IN WORLD ORDER

Christianity and the Race Problem 101
    GONZALO BÁEZ-CAMARGO

Economic Freedom 125
    JOHN B. CONDLIFFE

CONTENTS

The Land and Human Welfare 140
BJARNE BRAATOY

Politics and Human Welfare 161
VERA MICHELES DEAN

The Health of the World Community 179
CHARLES-EDWARD A. WINSLOW

Christianity and the Workers of the World 201
CARTER GOODRICH

Human Character and World Order 217
REINHOLD SCHAIRER

Biographical Notes 251

8

The Introductory Lecture

PRACTICAL RELIGION IN THE WORLD OF TOMORROW

HENRY A. WALLACE

Vice President of the United States of America

THERE ARE THREE GREAT PHILOSOPHIES IN THE WORLD TO-day. The first, based on the supremacy of might over right, says that war between nations is inevitable until such time as a single master race dominates the entire world and everyone is assigned his daily task by an arrogant, self-appointed Fuehrer. The second—the Marxian philosophy—says that class warfare is inevitable until such time as the proletariat comes out on top, everywhere in the world, and can start building a society without classes. The third—which we in this country know as the democratic Christian philosophy—denies that man was made for war, whether it be war between nations or war between classes, and asserts boldly that ultimate peace is inevitable, that all men are brothers, and that God is their Father.

This democratic philosophy pervades not only the hearts and minds of those who live by the Christian religion, both Protestant and Catholic, but of those who draw their inspiration from Mohammedanism, Judaism, Hinduism, Confucianism, and other faiths. When we look beneath the outer forms, we find that all these faiths, in one way or another, preach the doctrine of the dignity of each individual human soul, the doctrine that God intended man to be a good neighbor to his fellow man, and the doctrine of the essential unity of the entire world.

9

Those who think most about individualism preach freedom. Those who think most about unity, whether it be the unity of a nation or of the entire world, preach the sacred obligation of duty. There is a seeming conflict between freedom and duty, and it takes the spirit of democracy to resolve it. Only through religion and education can the freedom-loving individual realize that his greatest private pleasure comes from serving the highest unity, the general welfare of all. This truth, the essence of democracy, must capture the hearts of men over the entire world if human civilization is not to be torn to pieces in a series of wars and revolutions far more terrible than anything that has yet been endured. Democracy is the hope of civilization.

To understand the significance of these three philosophies dominant in the world today, let us look at each one in turn. During the last eighty years, the outstanding exponent of the sacredness and inevitability of war has been Prussia. By nature the common people of Prussia are simple and hardworking, and make excellent citizens except where they have become infected by the Prussian doctrine that might makes right. The Prussian philosophy causes its adherents to practice many of the highest virtues, but these virtues are all ultimately placed at the disposal of supreme evil. Hitler, seizing the Prussian militaristic tradition as a powerful instrument in his hands and putting it to use with his own religious frenzy, has become the antichrist of this generation—perhaps the most complete antichrist who has ever lived. It is not enough to bring about the downfall of Hitler. We must understand the origin and growth of the Prussian spirit, and do something to counteract that spirit, if we wish to bring permanent peace.

The Prussian attitude toward war and supremacy has strong roots. Whether it reaches back to the days of Caesar or whether it first took form under the guidance of the Teutonic knights in the Middle Ages, we are certain of this: by the time of Frederick the Great, the Prussians consciously adopted the doctrine of total war and the total state as the chief end of man. Bismarck and Kaiser Wilhelm II modernized and made completely deceitful and ruthless that which Frederick the Great had founded.

Shortly after Kaiser Wilhelm II rose to power, a generation before the first World War, one of the more tenderhearted of the German generals said, in addressing his troops: "Our civilization must build its temple on mountains of corpses, an ocean of tears, and the groans of innumerable dying men."

We know now, to our sorrow, that those were not just idle words. But God grant they will not be true much longer!

Bernhardi and Treitschke, through the printed page and through the classroom, preached the glory of war and the necessity of Germany's picking a quarrel with England or France. Frederick the Great, Moltke, and Bismarck were proclaimed as being superior to Goethe, Schiller, Bach, and Beethoven. Hegel laid broad and deep the philosophy of the totalitarian state. Other philosophers, and especially Nietzsche, seized on the Darwinian doctrines of natural selection and survival of the fittest to erect a seemingly scientific but false materialism to justify their ruthless acts.

In saying all of this I do not mean to indicate that Prussia was the only wicked state in the world. England, France, Russia, Spain, and the United States were not always perfect. But Prussia and Japan were the only countries which systematically devoted the highest virtues of their citizenry, generation after generation, to the glorification of the state and to the ruthlessness of war.

The ancestors of many of the people of German origin in the United States were members of the minority in

11

Germany who dissented from the extremist tendencies toward militarism. Thousands of these dissenters migrated to this country in the twenty or thirty years after the failure of the revolution of 1848. Their children, grandchildren, and great-grandchildren today are among our finest American citizens. They are patriotically doing their part in the present war for freedom, and we honor them for the spirit they have shown.

It is in the years since 1848 that the liberal culture of the old Germany has been so completely submerged by the worship of strength and power. In this period of less than a century, under Bismarck, Kaiser Wilhelm II, and Hitler, Germany has launched five aggressive wars.

The result has been that, over the last thirty years, the spirit of Prussianism has cost the lives of at least twenty million men, has crippled at least ten million others, and has caused the nations of the world to squander hundreds of billions of dollars on death, destruction, and hate. How different things would have been if this money had been spent instead on peace, prosperity, and understanding.

Germans by blood are neither better nor worse than Englishmen, Americans, Swedes, Poles, or Russians. But the Prussian tradition of the last century, and especially the Nazi education of the last ten years, have created a psychic entity so monstrous and so dangerous to the entire world that it is absolutely vital to exercise some control over German education when the war comes to an end. Prussian schoolmasters have been of greater importance to the German army than Prussian captains, and Prussian textbooks have had greater value than ammunition. It is the disciplined will to power and the worship of war as the method of power that have made the German army such a terrible instrument of force.

Just as Hitler took the Prussian military tradition and

12

organized it into gangsterism, so he took the Prussian educational system and streamlined it to marshal the millions of German boys and girls behind his evil conspiracy of world conquest. Hitler's children have been trained to believe implicitly that the state is more important than the individual, and that the individual must be willing and ready to sacrifice himself for the German nation and for the Fuehrer. Starting with the young mothers and fathers, married or unmarried, and taking the children through the day nurseries and a series of schools for different ages, Hitler has indoctrinated the German children with what he calls his "leadership principle"—that among men as in nature there is an eternal struggle between the weak and the strong, and that the "decadent" democracies are destined to crumble before the superior might of the Nazi elite. German boys have been systematically trained in brutality. German girls have been systematically trained to believe that their supreme duty is to be mothers, married or unmarried, of children dedicated to the service of the Fatherland and the Fuehrer. Through the use of mystic ceremonies—pagan dances, bonfires, sun festivals on mountaintops, and many other types of ritual—both boys and girls have been trained to look upon Hitler as divine, and they pray to him as God.

The evil influence of this systematic degradation of millions of German boys and girls cannot be counteracted in a short time. Even Hitler's death will not end it, because many of Hitler's children, conditioned as they are, will believe that he is still their leader. in the spirit if not in the flesh. Hitler dead may be almost as dangerous as Hitler alive.

This, then, is the vastly difficult problem with which the United Nations will have to cope if the victory which now is coming closer is to bring more than just a short breathing

HENRY A. WALLACE

spell before another Prussian attack is launched upon the world.

It is not up to the United Nations to say just what the German schools of the future should teach, and we do not want to be guilty of a Hitlerlike orgy of book burning. But it is vital to the peace of the world to make sure that neither Prussianism, Hitlerism, nor any modification of them is taught. There are many cultured German scholars with an excellent attitude toward the world who should be put to work on the job of rewriting the German textbooks in their own way. I believe these men would glorify peace and international honesty, re-establishment of the German culture of Beethoven, Schubert, Schiller, and Goethe, and the gradual preparation of the German spirit for an appreciation of the fact that a Bill of Rights for the individual is as vital as a Bill of Duties toward the state.

Doubtless thousands of German boys will come home from the war bitterly disillusioned because of Prussianism and Hitlerism. Thousands of both young and old at home will feel the same way. They will honestly want to help build up a new democratic Germany; and we, without yielding at all to the old warlike spirit of Prussia, should encourage them to try. We shall need the help of all Germans who give convincing evidence that they do not subscribe to the "master-race" myth and are genuinely opposed to the doctrine that might makes right. The re-education we insist upon should not crush out any sincere desire to practice democracy and live at peace among the world family of nations.

It will not be necessary for Americans to teach in German schools. The all-important thing is to see that the cult of war and international deceit is no longer preached as a virtue. We cannot countenance the soft, lazy forgetfulness which characterized England and France

14

in their treatment of Germany in the thirties. The cost of such short-sighted appeasement is too great in men and money. We must not go down that mistaken, tragic road again.

All of my discussion thus far has been concerned with Prussianism. Now I want to talk about Marxianism. This philosophy in some ways is the child of Prussianism, because Marx, its high priest, was molded in his thinking by Hegel, the great philosopher of the Prussian state. Marxianism has used the Cheka, just as Prussianism has used the Gestapo, but it has never preached international war as an instrument of national policy. It does not believe one race is superior to another. Many of the Marxian activities of the last ten years which people of the West have most condemned have been inspired by fear of Germany. The Russian people, who are the chief believers in Marxianism, are fundamentally more religious than the Prussians. The great mass of the Russian people is still hungry for spiritual food. The Russians have a better opportunity to find that spiritual food than have the Prussians under their regime, which glorifies the violence of the old Teutonic gods.

This question of religious freedom in Russia has been getting attention from the Church of England and from the Roman Catholic Church in this country. In a recent issue of the magazine *Commonweal,* which surely cannot be said to have Marxian leanings, the managing editor discussed two books by exiled Russians on the status of religion in Russia. Quoting from both books, one written under the auspices of the Church of England, and the other by a professor at Fordham University, the editor came to the conclusion that the position of the Christian church in Russia has definitely improved.

The future well-being of the world depends upon the extent to which Marxianism, as it is being progressively modified in Russia, and democracy, as we are adapting it to twentieth-century conditions, can live together in peace. Old-line Marxianism has held that democracy is mere words, that it serves the cause of the common man with platitudes rather than with jobs, and that belief in it results in a weak governmental organization· And we who believe in democracy must admit that modern science, invention, and technology have provided us with new bottles into many of which we have not yet poured the wine of the democratic spirit.

In some respects both the Prussians and the Russians have perceived the signs of the times better than we—and I hope that reactionary politicians will not quote this sentence out of its context, in an effort to prove that I have come out for dictatorship. The fact is that the Prussians have done an effective job of making their bureaucrats efficient in co-ordinating the social forces in the service of the state. The Russians have put great emphasis on serving and gaining the enthusiastic adherence of the common man. It is my belief that democracy is the only true expression of Christianity; but if it is not to let Christianity down, democracy must be tremendously more efficient than it has been in the service of the common man, and in resistance to selfish pressure groups.

After this war is over, the democratic capitalistic nations will need to prove that they are supremely interested in full employment and full utilization of natural resources. They will need to demonstrate that the consuming power of their people can be made to equal their productive power. The right to work at a regular job and for a decent wage is essential to the true dignity of man.

If the Western democracies furnish full employment and an expanding production, they need have no fear of a revival of old-line Communistic propaganda from within. If they do not furnish full employment, Communistic propaganda of this kind is inevitable, and there is nothing which the Russian government or our government or any other government can do to stop it. In the event of long-continued unemployment, the only question will be as to whether the Prussian or Marxian doctrine will take us over first.

I believe in the democratic doctrine—the religion based on the social message of the prophets, the heart insight of Christ, and the wisdom of the men who drew up the Constitution of the United States and adopted the Bill of Rights. By tradition and by structure we believe that it is possible to reconcile the freedom and rights of the individual with the duties required of us by the general welfare. We believe in religious tolerance and the separation of church and state, but we need to light again the old spirit to meet the challenge of new facts.

We shall decide sometime in 1943 or 1944 whether to plant the seeds for World War No. 3. That war will be certain if we allow Prussia to rearm either materially or psychologically. That war will be probable in case we double-cross Russia. That war will be probable if we fail to demonstrate that we can furnish full employment after this war comes to an end and Fascist interests motivated largely by anti-Russian bias get control of our government. Unless the Western democracies and Russia come to a satisfactory understanding before the war ends, I very much fear that World War No. 3 will be inevitable. Without a close and trusting understanding between Russia and the United States there is grave probability after this war is over of Russia and Germany sooner or later making common cause.

Of course the ground for World War No. 3 can be laid by actions of the other powers, even though we in the

17

United States follow the most constructive course. For example, such a war would be inevitable if Russia should again embrace the Trotskyist idea of fomenting world-wide revolution, or if British interests should again be sympathetic to anti-Russian activity in Germany and other countries.

Another possible cause of World War No. 3 might rise out of our own willingness to repeat the mistakes we made after World War No. 1. When a creditor nation raises its tariffs and asks foreign nations to pay up, and at the same time refuses to let them pay in goods, the result is irritation of a sort that sooner or later leads first to trade war and then to bloodshed.

The gospel of Christ was to feed the hungry, clothe the naked, comfort the sick, and visit those who were in hard luck. He said that treating your neighbor decently was the way to show that you loved God. The neighborhood in Christ's day was a few miles in diameter. Today the airplane has made the whole world a neighborhood. The Good-Neighbor policy, whether at home or abroad, is a Christian policy. Those who preach isolationism and hate of other nations are preaching a modified form of Prussian Nazism, and the only outcome of such preaching will be war.

If we want peace, we must treat other nations in the spirit of democratic Christianity. We must make our religion practical. In our relations with China, for example, we must act in such a way as to enhance the material as well as the spiritual well-being of her people. So doing will not only be of spiritual advantage to ourselves, will not only do much to prevent war, but will give us more material prosperity than we can otherwise enjoy. And in saying this I do not preach the missionary spirit as a fore-runner of a new imperialism.

Nearly half the people of the world live in Eastern Asia. Seven eights of them do not know how to read and write; but many of them listen to the radio, and they know that the world is on the move, and they are determined to move with it. We can at their request help them to move in knowledge toward a higher standard of living rather than in ignorance toward confusion and anarchy.

Throughout history every big nation has been given an opportunity to help itself by helping the world. If such an opportunity is seized with a broad and generous spirit, an infinitude of practical possibilities opens up. Thousands of businessmen in the United States have seen this kind of thing happen on a smaller scale in their own businesses, as their broad and enlightened policies have increased their prosperity and given jobs to their neighbors. Christianity is not stargazing or foolish idealism. Applied on a world-wide scale, it is intensely practical. Bread cast upon the waters does return. National friendships are remembered. Help to starving people is not soon forgotten. We of the United States, who now have the greatest opportunity that ever came to any people, do not wish to impose on any other race or to thrust our money or technical experts or ways of thought on those who do not desire them. But we do believe that if we measure up to the responsibility which Providence has placed on our shoulders, we shall be called on for help by many peoples who admire us. When we respond to this cry for help, we shall be not only manifesting a Christian spirit, but also obeying a fundamental law of life.

We of the Western democracies must demonstrate the practicality of our religion. We must extend a helping hand to China and India; we must be firm and just with Prussia; we must deal honestly and fairly with Russia, and be tolerant and even helpful as she works out her economic problems in her own way; we must prove that we ourselves can give an example, in our American democratic way, of full employment and full production for the benefit of the common man.

By collaborating with the rest of the world to put productive resources fully to work, we shall raise our own standard of living and help to raise the standard of living of others. It is not that we shall be taking the bread out of the mouths of our own children to feed the children of others, but that we shall co-operate with everyone to call forth the energies of everyone, to put God's earth more completely at the service of all mankind.

Fundamental Christian Principles

GOD AND THE WORLD WE LIVE IN

FRANCIS J. MCCONNELL

Resident Bishop of The Methodist Church in the New York Area

EVERY AGE SEEKS TO INTERPRET THE IDEA OF GOD ACCORDing to its highest moral standards. This does not necessarily mean that the idea of God develops as a mere deposit of what we call wishful thinking. "Wishful" has about it a suggestion of laziness. "Demands which come with thinking" is a better term, especially when we are considering moral demands. Inasmuch as belief in God is not demonstration, but belief, we may just as well set ourselves to believing a God worth believing in. This need not mean that we are shaping an idea of God as idea alone, without any regard to the reality of God. It may mean that through bringing our best moral understanding to the interpretation of God, especially in his relations to men, we are moving toward the real.

It is the aim of this lecture to stress the idea that a God who acts under moral responsibility in the use of power is the God we need for the world in which we live, and that the attempt to act as laborers together with such a God is the supreme duty for men at the present hour.

An outstanding demand in ethical thinking today sets itself for the union of power and responsibility. If a moral agent has no power, there is no use of talking about his responsibility. If he does have power, he works under

21

responsibility. Responsibility to whom? Responsibility to any mind which is able to form moral judgments.

There is some question today as to the extent of the power of God, especially in the moral sphere. We need not concern ourselves long with the threadbare debates about the absolute and the infinite to recognize the seriousness of some of the present-day debates about limitations of God. If God is the creator of free men, how far did he limit himself in granting such freedom? Has he made provision for the damage done in a world like ours by the misuse, and indeed the use, of this freedom? The creation of a race of free beings is the heaviest moral responsibility conceivable. In one way or another we have to face this problem of power and responsibility in the Divine if we are to get anywhere in fashioning our thoughts about God.

There are various attitudes taken toward the question today. One ignores the problem altogether by taking no attitude. Multitudes of presumably intelligent persons do not appear even to have thought of the union of power and responsibility at all. It may be that if the professed believers in God had taken their beliefs more seriously this indifference would not be so widespread.

There are others who say that the world is God's affair, indeed is none of our business. Some say that it is our business just to make adjustment to the world powers—find out what those powers want done and do it. This really is a survival of the notions of political absolutism which have come down to us from the Middle Ages. The king can do no wrong. Practically this notion as applied to rule over society had its merits. There had to be final authority somewhere. Even so, however, we know today as benefactors of mankind many who rebelled in their day against kings who made their kingly power an instrument of tyranny. There is nothing notably moral in making adjustment to physical necessity, sensible as that adjustment may be. We call such adjustment more definitely prudential than moral. We have all heard of the remark attributed to Thomas Carlyle when he heard that Margaret Fuller had decided to accept the universe: "Gad! She'd better!" This is usually supposed to be a happy hit by Carlyle, but it is happy only if the problem is one of prudence. When it comes to the higher values, however, some of the greatest saints have been the greatest rebels.

Another group, oppressed by the manifest extent of moral evil in the world, tell us that all the dark features of the universe are the consequence of human sin. There is closer connection of this view with that other Middle Ages idea of the strict demands of divine government of the Kingdom of God than we like to admit. The laws of Christendom during the Middle Ages seem to us, as we look back at them, to have had to do mostly with penalties; and when those laws were taken as sanctioned by the divine law, the result was often more suggestive of the diabolical than of the divine. In any case, we do not get far in the situation of the present day by thinking of men chiefly as sinners and of God as an adjuster of penalties. If every man on earth could this instant be converted to Christian good will, to genuine and wholehearted love for God and man, the longest single step toward a Kingdom of God on earth would have been taken, but there would still remain a mass of darkness to be dealt with. Some of the mystery might even be more acute.

Others again, and among them some of our most recent Christian philosophers, think our difficulty can be solved only by assuming that there are in the nature of God obstacles to any easy handling of the tasks set the universe, that to a degree God himself works under the law of development. Insisting, as these thinkers do, on the moral perfections of God, they maintain that in his own nature there are qualities which can come to expression only as God finds, or works, his way to a solution. This view calls for a good deal of explanation; and the explanation, illuminating as it often is, raises a swarm of stimulating but baffling questions.

Perplexed by all such enigmas there are today scores of good people who call themselves, and are called, humanists. This is not a new term. It is fair to speak of Erasmus as a humanist and of Comte as avowedly one. There are too many varieties of humanists today to mention, ranging all the distance from Christian believers to avowed atheists. However they may differ, in their philosophic views they are alike as making human beings the aim of their efforts. Most of them act in the spirit of Christianity. The sum total of good they render to men year by year is beyond estimate.

Still, the very fact of the presence not so much of evildoers in the world as of good-doers makes more insistent the consideration of the moral responsibility of God. I am of course here assuming a personal God, though what I am to say would apply to a belief like Matthew Arnold's in a "Power not ourselves that makes for Righteousness." On any other assumption what I am saying will make no sense at all, but on that assumption the responsibility for the divine use of power is inescapable if we are to think of God at all.

Let me call attention for a moment to the growth of recognition of the need of holding users of power responsible for what the moral sentiment of a time regards as the best possible result. Lest we seem to make this emphasis altogether too modern, let me say that we have only to go back to the Old Testament for as high a statement of this principle as any ever uttered. The entire Old

24

Testament, indeed, is written from the assumption of the need of divine responsibility in the use of power. "Shall not the judge of the earth do right?" I have in mind more especially, however, the insistence of the scriptural writers on the obligations of kings to their people. The encounter of Elijah with Ahab over Naboth's vineyard is a case in point, as is also the question of the northern tribes of Israel to Rehoboam as to whether he would be a king to them after the manner of a servant of the people. In addition are the denunciations of courts for unfair decisions, especially against the poor, of rich men who laid house to house and land to land till there was "no place." It would not be extreme to say that the offenses of men to one another in the abuse of privileged powers are among the most often mentioned in the Old Testament.

About all the wrongs rebelled against in the course of history have been the irresponsible uses of power. The list, of course, could not be more than mentioned. We must be content to think only of the growth of the insistence on social responsibility in our own day. In my boyhood the right of a man to run his business in his own way was seldom questioned; and when it was, the question was looked upon as unpatriotic, irreligious, incendiary, and crazy. Moreover, there was a gulf fixed which religious teachers were not supposed to try to cross—the chasm between the strictly personal, individual duties and those having to do with the social order. All these latter lay outside the Christian realm, and Christians were not supposed to raise the question as to the effects of these activities on social welfare. All of this has changed, is still changing, and is inevitably to change more rapidly in keeping with the realization of the truth that power is to be held responsible by society for its effects upon men, women, and children. Every human institution today—industrial, family, religious, political—every one involving human contacts has to face the question as to the effects on the people who have to live under it. Every institution has to look upon its power, or its permission to exercise its power, as a grant from society itself. Society itself has to test its own powers by the same ideals.

The idea of God has to meet the same test. There is a good deal of criticism of the liberalism of the last half century that is pertinent just now, though we admit that some criticism is not just at all. The liberalism that has stood for free speech and for free assembly has placed civilization under lasting debt, but the liberalism which has refused to look at all at the sternness of the universe in which we live is not to be so highly praised. The universe is a grim place if we look at both kinds of facts that confront us. It is not fair to represent Jesus as if he were a sunny, amiable person with his face always wreathed in smiles. He indeed said that not a sparrow falls to the ground without the notice of the Father in heaven. His stress was on the care of God: he knew as well as anybody that God is the author of the power that brings the sparrow down. His own life was tragedy. Also liberalism was at fault in speaking as if men, by yielding to an easy attraction, could stroll into the Kingdom of God. The way has been described as broad and the rough places all made smooth, the moral ascent so gradual as to call for hardly any climbing. It so has been evident enough that no other kingdom of the higher values has been quite this easy. The gates to the realms of science and art are still narrow.

It is perhaps well for our peace of mind that we do not trouble ourselves with much attention to long views either of space or time. When we think of the human race, we are not likely to look far. Taking the whole of the human race into the account, and the whole course of history, also, the fact probably is that up to date there has likely not been a day in history when the majority of mankind have lain down to rest at night having known through the day the satisfaction of enough to eat.

There are indeed some compensatory reflections, but they are not of decisive weight. We can take what comfort we can from Karl Marx's profound remark that human history, so far as the race is concerned, has not yet begun. This can guard against rashness of judging too soon; but the other part of the Marx teaching is not so comforting, namely, that it cannot begin until there is revolutionary change in the production of the earth's products and their distribution. Still there is some hope in the thought that the curtain of the world's drama has not yet been lifted.

Perhaps there is something worth thinking about also in the probability that the universe is not chiefly man-centered. That the earth is not the center of all things is clear enough, and it may well be that man has been fitted into cosmic relations as a plane for high training without the physical world's being exhausted in its significance by its relation to man. As a practical-minded theistic philosopher once said, "The earth is merely a hot-house frame in which to start the plants."

Now is it worth while to give expression at a time like this to so much agnosticism even if we insist that the agnosticism is Christian, or at least is stated with a Christian aim? I think there is, for questions like these come up at times like these, and it is dangerous to religious interests to put them aside or to ignore them. Even if we know that we cannot answer such questions, it is a duty to face them. A large part of wisdom shows itself in the willingness to

27

say frankly that we do not know. There is no use in brooding over the insoluble, but it is worth something to see what is insoluble. The church has too often in the course of its history hurt itself and its adherents by claiming to know what it does not know, and cannot know. Anyhow, it is always a help toward knowledge to recognize the limits within which the search for knowledge must move.

A great world crisis is before us, probably the most critical crisis of the kind the world has ever seen. There are two attitudes toward that crisis which do not give a good account of themselves when we are seeking to look at the divine with the responsibility for the use of power in mind. One is the assumption, no doubt for the most part not deliberate or intentional, that in September, 1939, the outbreak of the war took the Lord of the universe by surprise, if I may speak without meaning to be flippant. Since that time this assumption is that God has been contemplating the world in a condition of horror. Some who take this attitude seem to imply that God is a perfectionist, turning away from all that is morally imperfect. A belief like this gets us nowhere. Then there is the other extreme—that God is immanent in this world, in all its processes in such fashion and degree that we may well leave everything to him. All will come right in the end. This view is as worthless as the other.

The doctrine just mentioned is sometimes called the transcendence of God. This is not quite the usual phrasing of transcendence, which puts God out of reach of men, as far as any close relation is concerned. The usual doctrine professes to lay chief stress upon the awful holiness of God, making him all but inaccessible to man. The current doctrine is a good deal like fatalism from one angle and looks a good deal like reliance on force from another.

Whatever messages God has for us are in the Bible, of course, but the revelation has to be accepted without much regard to anything relative in the message itself or to the relativities in human lives. The absolute in human experience can be seized only by minds in the midst of all sorts of relativities in men's minds and in their conditions. The message of this transcendentalism is to take it or leave it, without much power to take or leave. We have to wait and see what the Divine will do. This is not usually stimulating. This transcendence is likely to transcend the moral law, which is an absurdity if our standard is that of thinking of the Divine as using power under moral responsibility.

This current notion of transcendence arises partly from an idea of immanence which had almost everything its own way through the half century closing perhaps five or ten years ago. That theory put God into everything, good or evil. Looked at from one point, its practical effect was almost the same as that of transcendence. In transcendence God does almost everything worth while, and in immanence God does everything. He is in the doings of men, in that they are phases of divine activity without any responsibility of their own—which reduces all things to the same moral level. This form of immanence makes the Divine immanent in moral evil, with no responsibility whatsoever. Surely God is transcendent in knowledge, and in aesthetic quality and moral fullness which we are not qualified to understand; and these qualities cannot be exhausted in any manifestations which we can now seize. God is immanent in everything except evil wills.

What we are striving to do here is to maintain that moral purpose is at work in the universe. This is assumption, to be sure, but an assumption that moral life calls for if we are to have a God at all. What is before us in this life if we cannot believe in moral purpose in the forces weaving and unweaving the universe? No doubt we shall be told to seek good for its own sake, holding fast to the good on its own reward. On this basis the problem of the good in the world becomes an even greater difficulty than the problem of evil once was. How did the good get into a world in which there is no possibility of free choice?

In the encounter with such questions there is no wonder that a worldly-wise man takes the cynic's advice to "cultivate a wise selfishness and a thick skin."

On the assumption that we are free beings the question then has to do with some further assumption as to the ways in which a God of responsibility must deal with free beings. I keep saying "assumption," because assumptions are the facts with which we have to do. If I seem to take too much time in speaking of assumption, I must plead that there is nothing more fruitful in thinking than a recognized assumption and nothing more dangerous than one not recognized. If we wait for absolute proof of freedom we shall not get far. If we choose to do so we may avow that freedom never has been formally proved, but in that case we may as well go further and say that for all we know, by demonstration without assumption, there may be no freedom. I do not know that there is anything in strict logic to forbid one's saying that the world is full of illusions, freedom among them. We may be so created, or evolved, that we think we are free when we are not. There are occasions in life when we do think we are free when we are not. If one chooses to ask if this illusion is not true with us always, there is nothing in logic to profit us. For all we know, so far as syllogistic demonstration is concerned, we may all be "puppets jerked by unseen wires." Indeed, there have been plenty of books written from the time when writing first began to show that the

30

universe is either a tragedy or a joke in that the inhabitants think themselves free—in which plight the books themselves have to be treated as jokes, even if we call them grim jokes. A part of the joke is that the authors write on the assumption that nobody will take their utterances with enough seriousness to accept them as a guide in life. If such views were thus accepted, life would hardly be worth living for anybody.

If we are to have a world of persons endowed with freedom, however, there will have to be appropriate stage for freedom, and appropriate setting. The common sense of the world recognizes that there is no use of talking about free choices in a world where the choice is made under compulsion. Promises exacted under threat are not binding. The conditions of a man's existence may be such as to do away with any of the thoughtfulness out of which a rational choice comes. The moral agent may be too hungry, or too cold, or too tired to care much about what choices he makes. We are all aware that our freedom is limited by the physical world in which we live. The earth is but a speck in the universe, and no matter how vaulting our ambition, there is no way of ever getting off that speck. All such limitations we recognize as inherent in the earthly conditions under which we live, but I am thinking now of hindrances which are conceivably remediable.

We do not always give enough heed to the truth that before we can have even approximately a Christian civilization we must have a social basis for that civilization. The situation is somewhat parallel to that necessary before animal and human life could appear on the earth. There had to be what Professor Henderson has called fitness of the environment. It will be recalled that some twenty-five years ago Professor L. J. Henderson wrote an illuminating book showing how delicately the properties of matter in the universe had to be adjusted to one another before there could be even a start toward biological progress. Any upset in the properties would make impossible the appearance of any life whatsoever. Similarly in the human realm some fixities have to be achieved if anything like Christian civilization is to have a chance. There must be something of social order, some reliance upon good will among men, some confidence that men usually speak the truth to one another—not with scientific accuracy it may be, but without intention to deceive—some respect on the part of men toward one another. If the society goes far enough to train itself to educational development, there must be regard for, and respect for, the principles which are indispensable to any educational advance—freedom to think, to question established beliefs and institutions, to publish results, to work with some degree of security as to livelihood.

To take an illustration from the history of Christianity itself, we have all heard many times that Jesus came in "the fullness of time." It may of course be that in the use of this phrase the scriptural writer was thinking of detailed fulfillment of particular Hebrew prophecies; but, prophecy apart, it is obvious that there had to be immense and agelong preparation for Jesus. In the terms in which we are now thinking, there had to be the veritable creation of a nation, the schooling of that nation through thousands of years, the working out of a system of laws aimed at the increase of human value and welfare, the work of the prophets and the seers. As for the supreme commandment of Jesus about loving God with heart and strength and mind and one's neighbor as oneself, both parts of the expression had been worked into expression before Jesus appeared. Jesus gave them imperishable force;

but the law was the outcome and product of centuries of thought, feeling, and experience in the career of Israel itself. If we take seriously this expression, "the fullness of time," we have to conclude that if Jesus had come too soon, his teaching and life would have got an inadequate start, and if there had been no preparation at all, there would have been no Christianity.

All of this leads to the reflection that a basis must be kept under Christianity. If there is attack upon the principles of order, upon the value of human beings in themselves, upon regard for truth-speaking and fair dealing, civilization has to give attention to strengthening the bases of civilization in the interest of civilization itself, and such defense of civilization is at the same time a defense of Christianity. The spokesmen for Christianity may protest that they do not want such defense, and the defenders of these foundations may not think of defending Christianity at all; but the defense is moral, nevertheless, and is one phase of the task of making possible the sway of moral considerations in human society. There may dawn a day when the mere utterance of the highest truth will sustain Christianity, but speaking for our own latitude and longitude and period in the world's history we may be permitted to say that the day has not yet dawned. Unceasing vigilance is the price of liberty in the religious sphere as well as elsewhere, and "elsewhere" must sooner or later include all the other spheres of human experience. If God is responsible for the moral significance of human society, and if human freedom comes as a gift from him, this can mean only that a God for the world in which we live must seek the moral co-operation of men in working out the conditions which give moral living its chance.

We are speaking from the point of view of the Christian revelation. If we accept the moral ideal of Jesus, we

cannot stop short of the ideal of moral perfection in our
thought of God himself and as the ideal of human conduct. The ideal of moral perfection did not come originally from Jesus. The pursuit of such perfection was a
fact of human experience long before the day of Jesus.
What Jesus did was to preach unqualifiedly the moral
quality of God, putting the capstone on the long progress
of the Hebrews toward making moral the conception of
the Divine. Jesus did not state with any detail what the
moral obligations of the divine Father involved, but he
made one piercing statement: Men are to be perfect even
as the Father in heaven is perfect. The mark of perfection is that God sends sunshine and rain upon the just and
the unjust alike, without favoritism. Men do not have
control of the rainfall and sunshine; so this concrete illustration does not point to anything that men can directly imitate; but this does not mean that the ideal can be dismissed as out of reach. The ideal gets near to earth though
men have not the power which reaches to the clouds or
to the sun. This word definitely is of material things and
of the right use of power. It is significant that Jesus used
this type of illustration to set the ideal on high. It would
have had but little meaning if Jesus had merely told his
disciples to be perfect as the Father in heaven is perfect
and had left the ideal thus in the air. Even the least of his
followers had some control over material goods and in the
use of these had to be faithful to the moral requirement
of impartial and even extravagant good will.

The further question at once arises to one anxious to
take this demand of good will seriously. Clearly the law
of good will is absolute. There cannot in the man of good
will be the slightest slackening of hold in the moral absolute. Lofty moral purpose discerned that long before
the coming of Jesus. The difficulty has always been in

34

the application of the law, in the relative use of the absolute. Suppose, to use a somewhat grotesque illustration, man could be given control over the sunshine and the rainfall. Just how, with the utmost good will, could he use it without perfect knowledge as well as complete good will? Myriads of practical considerations would come up at once. It is so in the pettiest concerns of our little lives. Just how to use what power we have to carry out the law of good will is a perennial problem. We often say that a perfectly just law has never been passed. We refer, of course, not to the spirit of the law but to the provisions for its actual working. The best we can hope for is as close approximation to justice as may be possible in the tangled, complex, and always changing world in which we have to live.

Some months ago Dr. Temple, the Archbishop of Canterbury, in speaking of the problem of the absolute and the relative, said that at times the relative becomes the absolute. If we pull ourselves clear of the etymological quibbles about the dictionary meanings of the terms, the Archbishop's suggestion is most helpful. In any crisis where a serious moral issue arises the relative must be taken as the absolute. It is only through the relative that the absolute can come into expression at all. The relative is the near side of the absolute.

Psychologically the furore in the past quarter century over the doctrine of relativity is one of the oddest events in the history of thought. The reason seems to be that the Einstein doctrine fell in with a mind of the time, with impatience as to universal and absolute laws. The commotion certainly did not arise from scientific reasoning strictly speaking. Multitudes of those who seemed relieved when told that Einstein's relativity had superseded Newton's laws had not the slightest idea of the

35

Newtonian system, to say nothing of the Einstein reasonings. Indeed, Einstein himself was seeking a new law which would have wider sweep than any of Newton's—even more inclusive than the Newton statement of gravitation. No, the temper was to get rid of all absolutes, especially those which seemed to bind our daily conduct. The relative seemed to provide a relief and ease, a result which was not contemplated in the Einstein formulation. For the mere understanding of Einstein, for the mere following his argument along requires a more thorough equipment than Newton himself had at hand.

Scientific thinking apart, the moral duty is to estimate and act upon the relative aright, for the relative is the only channel through which the absolute can reach us or we can reach the absolute. It would be doing violence to the teaching of Jesus and to the moral law itself to assume that moral relativity leaves everything at loose ends. Suppose Jesus had said, "Be perfect," and nothing more; the law would have been left just where it was before. If he had said, "You are to have a hard time in following me. Do the best you can and let it go at that," Christianity as such might never have been. He did teach that men are to do the best they can as they aim at a perfect ideal. Men are not to live along by rule of thumb without seeking perfection. They are to take the pursuit of perfection seriously as they do the best they can from day to day.

This will not please the perfectionists as we ordinarily use the term—the moralists who insist upon following the absolute literally, unqualifiedly, without any reservation whatsoever. Such absolutists have their place—and important place in a moral community—as thrusting the absolute constantly upon our attention. The radical absolutist, however, is much like all other absolutists; he is likely to be a specialist, and the specialist seldom sees a wide field. His mind itself is relative to the one part of his universe which absorbs his attention at the time, and he pours all his energy through one outlet.

In a word, the teaching of Jesus is that in God the ideal is real. If this is true, the ideal is not a dream or a product of imagination, but a fact to be taken account of as other realities must be.

One difficulty with the idealist who has no keen awareness of the realities of actual life is that when he has said a thing he thinks he has done it. Doing the full moral duty calls for something more than saying. Expression of moral conviction in any situation calls for the activity of the will. Christianity is above all other religions a religion of the will. It may be said that here is part of the claim of Christianity to be a religion for all men. Not all men can understand doctrine. Not all have the mystic temperament. But all normal persons can do something to show response to the good. The activity of the will is the path toward religious knowledge and toward religious feeling. Pragmatism may deserve much of the criticism it gets when taken as itself a system of knowledge, but it never can be praised enough as a method in the search for knowledge. Knowledge and feeling, to be real in any effective degree, come out of doing. Something of this was what the Christian teachers of an earlier day seem to have had in mind when they said so often that Christian certainty comes out of Christian experience. Any man who can do anything can do something toward learning the values of the moral kingdom.

I am speaking of the methods by which the absolute moral ideal can be made real in human experience. The relative in the moral life confronts us also in the fact of change, or process. The fact that confronts us is not necessarily progress but process. Progress as an aim is of comparatively recent date in human society. This does not mean that there has not been progress, but not until comparatively recently has progress been taken as a principle on its own account to be spelled with a capital and treated with something resembling intellectual and emotional worship. The two world wars have pretty well disposed of that fancy. That there is change in social movement nobody can deny, but that the change is progress is doubtful. At least the doctrine that progress is inevitable is doubtful. Indeed, it begins to appear that if we can ever get to the place where there can be said to be any such reality as a world-wide public moral sentiment, the chief task of this sentiment will be so to direct change as to ensure progress.

At times the stream of human history seems to become a maelstrom, with the current swirling round and round, with no power to break out of the circle. If it is declared that such problems are beyond us, we do not especially honor the moral God. If through no fault of our own we have to whirl constantly with no chance to get ahead, the conception of moral progress is somewhat of a mockery. It would be a mockery, too, if we were to think of a moral God in indulgent fashion as transforming all social movements to make them move toward righteousness without our help. Indeed, one of the most hopeful signs of moral health at the present hour is the discussion of plans for the betterment of the human race. Some of these plans are not wisely conceived, but the prevalence of discussion about them is stimulating. World-wide attacks on diseases which have been with the race from the beginning are both fact and symbol of the moral temper which is willing to try out the moral energy on all

38

manner of scourges which have been hanging on the flank of humanity from the beginning.

Or take the scourge of war. Here is a plague which has been upon nations, virtually all of them, through the ages, constantly spreading and always more deadly. One group has proposed to stand above it, insisting with energy, not to say vehemence, that no war has ever been productive of any good, out of an unreal and unhistoric temper that whatever good we suppose has come from war could have better come through some other channel, a proposition unassailable enough if the world of men and things could have been altogether different from what it has been. Another group will have it that war has always been with us and always will be. Between these groups an increasing multitude is approaching the problem with a more realistic mind than either of the other two groups and seeking nothing short of a world-wide social organization which will make war obsolete.

This growing willingness to think in world terms is the distinctive moral mark of our times. It is easy enough to say that we face evils which are apparently fixed in the constitution of society and that our moral fiber is to show itself in the patience with which we put up with them. We have heard about taking up our arms against a sea of troubles and by opposing ending them, but we have through the ages had but little thought of ending them. We have assumed that ending them is as impossible as stopping the waves of the sea by opposing them. Moral heroism that stands against these world-wide evils and protests against them till we go down has seemed the sturdiest of virtues. "Sweet are the uses of adversity" has seemed a worthy consolation, and "A smooth sea makes a poor sailor" wise advice. The moral truth is becoming clearer day by day that if we have any power over the world-wide forces which make for adversity we have responsibility also.

To glance at an example from the economic world, we have to recognize that the economic world is more and more a unity. That fact means that the whole world is subject together to the rhythmic or cyclic booms and depressions which at more or less regular intervals lift the world into artificial prosperity and depress it into almost bottomless abysses. There are those among us who say that this is in the nature of things and that we had better make the most of the prosperity while it lasts in order to carry on through the depression that follows. With depressions that come from uncontrollable natural calamities we do indeed have to adjust ourselves as best we can, but most of the world-wide depressions are man-made. Not that men deliberately make them, but men make them, nevertheless. A tariff imposed by a majority of Congress, let us say by six hundred votes, affects in some degree the welfare of one hundred million Americans and may put an entire industry in Europe out of business. The votes of the six hundred may have been determined by the recommendations of a committee of fifty, and the opinions of a half dozen alleged experts may have convinced the fifty. A decision as to the exchange rate of currencies between two nations may economically ruin one nation or perhaps cripple both. To be sure, we are told that in all such relations we are dealing with impersonal laws of supply and demand and so on and on, ignoring the fact that men make the demand and men make the supply. When enough men take seriously the responsibility which comes with the incalculable power of national control over production and distribution, economic cycles can be robbed of at least half their devastating terror.

I have been trying to say that the idea of God which we should seek to enforce today is one which carries on further toward the moralization of our theology by laying emphasis on responsibility in the use of power, and that the path toward communion with a moral God is just now to seek to be laborers together with God in such moral effort. Speaking for our own nation, we have now greater power than any other nation has ever had. The progress of events is compelling us to think of the use of that power in racial terms. If we are to think of a Kingdom of God at all today, we must think in racial terms, as only a handful of human beings now and again has tried to do at all so far as the higher human values are concerned. The economic power is here and is being used. The problem is to create a policy of togetherness which will make possible a separateness of national development that will give each people a chance at its highest and best life.

Some things in this world of ours have to be done by the peoples working together, or they will not, and cannot, be done at all. Take disarmament. If three out of four great nations of the world agree to disarm and one other nation with any considerable power at all continues to arm, the disarmament of the three will only make the international situation worse. Fervid national declarations of the duty of one nation's taking the lead in disarmament have been reduced to the thinnest of thin air by the history of the world during the last decade. If war is to be outlawed, measures will have to be taken in grim earnest to make the international criminal industry unprofitable. The difficulty here is that while we have preached the duty of the responsibility of a privileged individual for the right use of his privileges, we have not attained to a realization of a nation's responsibility for its privileges. If we are to be Christian at all in our idea of God, we have to think of God as of the whole race. This consideration, utterly commonplace as it is, will have to be given the force of an actual discovery soon if civilization is to live on at more than a poor, dying rate. There is no going back to the day when a nation could live by itself. There are no walls that can shut out air approach. It may well be that a nation's first duty is to its own citizens, and it surely is true that each nation is entitled to live out its distinctive destiny; but each nation's interest can best be cared for by international relationships which make it possible for the nations to do together what they can best do together, leaving them free to do separately what they can best do separately. If democracy is what we claim that it is, rooted or at least implied in Christian revelation, we have to think of the welfare of the masses of mankind as the chief object of divine concern. The coolness with which the present nations and churches of Christendom assume that they are the supreme objects of divine care is amazing when you reflect that the majority of the human race now and in the past has been outside the so-called Christian circle.

There is a practical view of history today that looks upon the so-called backward races as having been useful in an instrumental sense, as having through their labor made possible the accumulation of wealth for the so-called higher classes and the enjoyment of leisure out of which scientific and artistic and philosophic achievement has come. We are told that if it had not been for slavery in ancient Greece, we might not have had the Parthenon and the incomparable masterpieces of statuary, that virtual slave labor also made possible the chivalry of feudalism, that the availability of cheap labor has been indispensable in the material development of civilization since the beginning of the Industrial Revolution. There is no way of going back and reliving the past, but that does not change the fact that the gains were purchased at tremendous cost. We are grateful that the spirit of our age is set against such appalling human costs for the benefit of any privileged persons, or group, or nation, or race. We must believe that the universe is one, that the race is one, and that any high ethics must think of moral responsibility in terms of the whole race.

We meet now a protest which in some minds has all along been struggling for utterance, to the effect that after all moral responsibility is an affair of persons, and individual persons at that, that all this emphasis on social points of view does not get down into that inner realm of freedom which is the center of moral life. To which we reply that no man lives to himself alone, that moral development never could take place except in the contacts of men with one another, that the growth of a social atmosphere which is the product of the interaction of moral wills is a mighty aid to the moral responses of individuals. The responsibility of men for their power is nowhere greater than in the use of this power to create a sentiment which looks outward from the smaller sphere, bringing more and more men within the range of our social duties, and looks inward from the idea of the larger sphere—the duty of making the idea of the whole moral universe lend dignity and might to the stirrings of the individual will.

I hardly need add that the force of Christian morality comes from accepting as divine revelation the view of men central in the teaching and life of Jesus Christ. We are all talking today about global war and global social re-organization and global material needs. The people of the time of Jesus would not have known what the word global means. The world to them was flat. The progress of the realization that the world is not a flat plain but a globe has not set aside but rather increased the knowledge of the moral world. A globe is a unity. The Creative Mind has

43

to treat it as a unity. The race that lives upon the globe is fundamentally one. The moral law that governs the globe must be one. The responsibilities of the Creator toward the race which he has created must treat the race as one. It is said that Abraham Lincoln, after hearing a lecture on immortality which declared that some races are too inferior to be given a chance at immortality, shook his head and said, "It must be all or none." So indeed it must, if the control of the globe is moral. So indeed it must be in men's thought of one another. Taking Jesus as the supreme revelation of the moral purposes of the Divine, we are convinced that his teaching of divine and human responsibility for the use of power becomes even more binding. Lincoln's word was, "It must be all or none." The teaching of Jesus means that moral opportunity must be for all. The passage from a flat world to a global world or to any kind of world revealed by science does not diminish the responsibility of God to men, or of men to God, or of men to one another.

THE CHRISTIAN CONCEPTION OF MAN

Willis J. King

President of Gammon Theological Seminary, Atlanta, Georgia

ONE OF THE MOST PRESSING AND, AT THE SAME TIME, most baffling problems of our day is a satisfactory view of the worth and dignity of man and his place in the scheme of things. What is man's relation to God, to the world of nature, to his fellow men? To what extent is his destiny predetermined, or is there freedom of choice? What worthy goals, if any, may he hope to achieve that make worth while the ceaseless struggle necessary for his continued existence? What are the possibilities for good will and co-operation among various racial and national groups in the achievement of worthy goals? To what extent, if any, may man have the help of Higher Powers to assist him in his struggles to achieve the higher life, granted that there is such a life? What is to be man's ultimate destiny?

These are some of the questions which thoughtful men are asking and the problems for which they are trying to find a solution. These problems are all the more urgent in a crisis such as mankind is passing through at the present time, involving tremendous sacrifices in the way of human life among all the peoples of the world. Adherents of the Christian faith believe they have in the Hebrew-Christian tradition the answer to these questions. It has been the task of Christian thinkers in every generation to attempt to interpret to their particular generation the Christian conception of man, as taught by the Scriptures, in relation to the problems of their own day. It is the conviction of this writer that only in the Scriptures do we have an authentic guide for an understanding of the Christian conception of man, and that while of course the biblical material comprising symbolic, narrative, doctrinal, and other types of literature will have to be interpreted in the light of changing conceptions of truth, particularly from the various fields of scientific endeavor, nevertheless the basic principles about man and his relation to God and the universe are to be found in the Christian revelation as set forth in the Holy Scriptures.

It will be the aim of this lecture to outline briefly the teachings of the Scriptures concerning man and to make an effort to apply these basic scriptural principles to our present-day situations. Before proceeding to this task, however, it may not be amiss to study critically some very definite views which are in competition with the Christian view and to note briefly the efforts of certain groups of modern Christian thinkers to meet the situation posed by the scientific developments of the modern world.

I. SOME MODERN COMPETING VIEWS

1. *The Mechanistic or Scientific Doctrine of Man*

One of the most persistent of the modern ideologies which has been in competition with the Christian world view has been called by some the "scientific doctrine of man," by others the "mechanistic view of the universe." Its basic concept is that man can be adequately explained by the ideas and principles of the natural sciences. This view rests on two principles, the principle of continuity and the principle of unity. The principle of continuity is the idea that whatever is found in nature and in history has

46

developed gradually from lower forms to higher. The principle of unity is the idea that ours is a unitary world and all being, including man, hangs together and comes under one order—the spiritual rests on the physical and is bound up with it. Darwin's theory of evolution seemed to be a confirmation of the view. Man comes, by this view, not from God but from the lower order of animal life. Further researches in biology and chemistry seemed to make the physical more basic as the place of man's origin.

The background of this view is the remarkable progress of mankind in the field of the natural sciences during the past few centuries. Scientists like Galileo, Kepler, and Newton and their modern counterparts have by their discoveries made for us not only a new world but a universe vastly more immense than the old world described by the author of Genesis. Our earth, which in the old view was the center of the universe, is now known to be a relatively small planet in our much larger solar system. Our sun, which is a million times larger than the earth, is but one of fifteen hundred million suns that compose the Milky Way. When one adds to this vastly enlarged universe these two principles—of continuity in development from the lower to the higher forms of life, and of unitary order, according to which both the physical and the spiritual would seem to have a common basis of origin—one would seem to have a strong argument for the dominance of the physical.

It is one thing, however, to recognize the achievements of science in giving us a new physical universe; it is an entirely different matter to deduce a world view on the basis of science. There are those who would make an issue between science and religion, but these two great servants of mankind are not necessarily antagonistic. The scientific and the religious interpretations of the universe are reached from distinct points of view and by different methods. The two are really complementary to each other. But a distinction must be made between the conclusions of science working in its legitimate field and the assumptions of a scientific creed based on an illicit extension into the fields of philosophy and religion. The sciences have to do with the description of the process by which development takes place; the background and origin of these processes are the domain of philosophy and religion.

Christian thinkers do not compete with science in its attempts to explain how the human race came into existence, or the stages of its evolution. Their chief concern is the nature and destiny of man. Whence came he and whither is he bound? They believe that in the Hebrew-Christian tradition are to be found the most satisfactory answers to these questions.

2. *Marxian Communism*

Another view which, since World War I, when it was taken over by Soviet Russia as its official view of the world and life, has become a keen competitor with the Christian world view is Communism, as set forth by Karl Marx and his associates. The Marxian conception of life can be appreciated only as one realizes that it emerged as a protest against the abstractions of certain German idealistic philosophers. In this connection it has rendered a distinct service. It has helped to clarify the philosophic picture as it relates to man himself. It has helped to emphasize the fact that, for mankind at least, the problem of man is of far greater importance than such abstract questions as time, space, and causality. It has focused attention upon the function of laboring with one's hands, and the difference in the labor situation made by tools and technical equipment. Finally, it has made clear the need for a radical reconstruction of society in the interest of exploited social classes.

48

In spite of its praiseworthy contribution to the socio-economic outlook of mankind, there are some definite and positive objections to Marxism: (*a*) The Marxian view is a materialistic-naturalistic point of view. According to Marx, man is the product of physical nature, and yet is to be thought of as having the lordship over nature. (*b*) Marxist teachings regard man as the sum total of socio-economic relations, leaving no place for such ideas as responsibility, inner spiritual life, ethical autonomy. (*c*) Marxism tends to identify, too completely, the individual with the universal. This means the absorption of the individual into the community. While it recognizes the individual as a unit in the community, it is the community rather than the individual which really matters. In Christianity each individual has inherent value in his own right. (*d*) Marxism is lacking in the proper appreciation of the place of religion in human life. It conceives of religion as an "opiate of the people." As over against this attitude is the Hebrew-Christian sentiment expressed by the psalmist: "As the hart panteth after the water brooks, so panteth my soul after thee, O God." Mankind, so the Christian believes, is incurably religious. Religion is a fundamental part of his nature. It is as native to him as the air he breathes, or the food he eats. Moreover, it is God's greatest gift to man—this longing for the higher life, and the conviction that it can be attained.

3. *The Totalitarian Nation-State*

Another type of competitor with the Christian world view is the totalitarian nation-state. This type of state is an autocracy whose leader or his representatives are the absolute authority. This state does not exist primarily for the benefit of its citizens, but uses them for the selfish purpose of the leaders. It is totalitarian in the sense that all the

49

agencies of the state, political, social, religious, are under the complete control of the state. Here even the church must be subordinated to the state, and the state determines what type of message may be preached and the character of religious instruction to be given. Moreover, loyalty to the state is given a mystical connotation which makes this loyalty supreme. Such a state acknowledges no law of God or truth or justice or mercy as being superior to it. The only law it recognizes is its own will and the measure of force it can command.

The example par excellence, at the moment, of the totalitarian state is the Nazi-controlled state of Germany. Here is to be found the ideology described above—namely, the absolute authority of the leader; supreme loyalty to the state, even in matters of religion; a low conception of the individual man, including the state's own subjects, who are regarded as merely its instruments; and a crude doctrine of racial supremacy, as far as other racial and national groups are concerned.

With the purely political forms of these Fascist experiments in government, Christian thinkers are relatively little concerned, as long as these nations do not seek either to dominate other peoples politically or to impose upon others their particular type of political and social views. But the Christian church can never compromise with a type of state which would make loyalty to it superior to loyalty to God. Further, it cannot tolerate any glorification of the state, or the community, which fails to recognize and respect the worth and dignity of the individual man. Nor can it put the stamp of its approval upon a concept of race which would completely obliterate the doctrine of the fatherhood of God and the brotherhood of all men.

50

THE CHRISTIAN CONCEPTION OF MAN

II. Some Modern Christian Views

1. *Religious Humanism*

One of the most interesting efforts of modern Christian thinkers to bring philosophy and religion into conformity with the scientific approach is what is known as religious humanism. Here two types may be distinguished: the psychological, with its development of subjective theories of religion; the sociological, with its emphasis on social idealism. Ludwig Feuerbach, a German pupil of Hegel, was the first to emphasize this psychological approach. He insisted that man can never get beyond his own nature. His consciousness of God is the self-consciousness of man, and his knowledge of God is the self-knowledge of man. When man worships God, he worships himself. The positive worth of religion is that it values qualities of life so highly. These qualities have been projected by man into a Divine Being outside of man. Religion is the dream of the human mind.

There is, of course, an element of truth in this point of view, as Dr. Rall reminds us, since "all our perceiving and thinking, all our interpretation of the world outside of us, must be after the analogy of something that we find within us." [1] But it must be kept in mind that our world is one world and is interrelated in a unitary working order. Man's moral and religious nature and the ideas they express have a valid place in that order.

The religious humanists whose approach is sociological are primarily social idealists whose social passion has led them to overemphasize the human aspect in the effort to correct what they believe to be an overemphasis on the Godward side. In some cases this has led them to be anti-

[1] Harris Franklin Rall, *Christianity* (New York: Charles Scribner's Sons, 1941), p. 273.

theistic, in others merely to ignore the theistic aspect in order to set forth the possibilities of man. An example of this type of humanist is Max C. Otto, whose position is set forth in his book *Things and Ideals*. Otto appreciates the value of science as the agency which gives man a knowledge of his physical environment, but insists that man must develop a higher life. In the achievement of this higher life man must make use of science and religion to aid him in his quest. He would, however, have mankind give up the quest for companionship with Higher Powers and assume that the universe is indifferent toward the human venture, that we are adrift in infinite space on our little earth and are dependent upon ourselves alone for salvation. He would have men develop a new sense of human solidarity and together build on the earth the fair city for which they have looked in the world beyond.

This desirable goal of human togetherness and human solidarity of which Otto writes is a lovely sentiment, and one to which unanimous agreement will be voiced, as far as the goal itself is concerned. There are relatively few Christian thinkers, however, who will agree that it can be achieved in the way suggested by Otto. Thus far the history of human relations where man has followed his own impulses without the guidance of Higher Powers has been based on the law of the jungle. It has been the rule of tooth and claw. The only hope for this human togetherness and solidarity of which Otto writes is the doctrine of the fatherhood of God and the brotherhood of all men as set forth in the Christian way of life, and the recognition of the need of divine help in the attainment of this ideal.

2. *The Neo-Orthodox Group*

One of the most striking, not to say violent, reactions against humanism is what is called by some neosupernaturalism, by others neo-orthodoxy. Modern thought had discovered the human side of religion. It was able to show that all the institutions of religion had come through a human and historical process, but religion had found man only to lose God.

Karl Barth, a Swiss pastor who had been trained under Hermann and the liberal Ritschlian school in Germany, and who was a religious socialist, with a faith that socialism was the hope of mankind, was disillusioned by World War I and its aftermath of world depression. He saw that man, the lordly creature who by his scientific prowess had conquered the world of nature and made himself the master of it, was himself the victim of his own machinery. Despite his tools and skills, man was powerless to avert the collapse of the civilization he had built.

Barth and his friends saw the war as a judgment upon the Christianity which had identified itself too much with the material interests with which it was surrounded. They were thrown back on the Bible and began to interpret it in a new light. They came to doubt the value of causes to which man gave his energies for the sake of his control over life. The Bible was the Book about God and his reality. It was concerned with human experiences and human enterprises only as they were related to God and his work in the world. God is God, not man. Man cannot control God. God controls man. Any form of human self-sufficiency is illusory. Man must recognize the failure of all his analyses and solutions. Only when men realize their utter inadequacy and complete failure is there any hope of salvation. That hope is Jesus Christ, who is the Word of God to man.

The Barthian school made a contribution by their protest against the religious agnosticism known as humanism, and in their rediscovery of the transcendence of God. But

in the words of one of his warmest admirers, "Barth is not
the prophet of the New Christianity. . . . . His voice rings
in our ears, and we will not forget his message, but we must
wait for another." [2] In his effort to exalt the claims of God
for sovereignty, Barth went to the extreme in underrating
man. The psalmist had a more balanced estimate: man is
but little lower than God himself. This is in harmony with
Jesus' conception of the worth and dignity of man.

III. What May We Believe About Man?

What, it may be asked, can Christians believe about man
in the light of the new world picture developed by science?
First it must be frankly recognized that the conception of
man's origin as set forth in Genesis is not a scientific statement of man's beginnings on the earth. It is rather a fundamental truth stated in poetic language, and in the framework of the scientific notions current in the period in which
its Semitic author or authors lived. The essential truth,
however, about man and his relation to God and the universe is, we believe, set forth in this and other parts of the
sacred scriptures of the Hebrew-Christian tradition. Moreover, it is interesting to note that the trend of science today is in the direction of recognizing the fact "that our
cosmos is an organic whole, not a chance conglomeration,"
and that man cannot be explained in terms of matter. It
is here that the insight of the biblical writers is to be found.

1. Man the Creature, God the Creator

The Hebrew writers were clear in their conviction that
man was neither self-created nor merely the sum total of
the physical and chemical elements which make up his
physical structure. Man the creature could be understood

[2] Wilhelm Pauck, *Karl Barth: Prophet of a New Christianity?* (New
York: Harper & Brothers, 1931), p. 220.

only as he was seen in relation to God the Creator. Man was meant to have dominion over the things which God had made, but man was lower than God and, in the presence of the holy God, could only think of himself as an unworthy creature. Man was absolutely dependent upon God for his existence and ultimate sustenance. It was the all-wise God and providential Father of mankind who stored the earth with abundant resources and created the conditions of soil, sunshine, and moisture which make possible continued and abundant life on the earth for man. This was the conviction of the writers of Holy Writ and may well be our view.

Further, God must be seen as the Lord of the universe and as the ultimate determinant in the history of mankind. Men are to be seen as having a place in the plan of God for the world, with the possibility of sharing in his righteous purpose. Indeed, God cannot achieve his righteous purpose for the world and for mankind without man's cooperation. To that extent God is dependent upon man, but ultimately it is God's purpose which is to be realized in the world. He may be delayed in the achievement of his purpose, either by the short-sightedness of man, or by his stubbornness, or by both; but ultimately God's righteous purpose for mankind and for the world will be achieved.

2. *Man a Combination of the Physical and the Spiritual*

The biblical writer not only saw man in his relation to God, but recognized him for what he is, an animal plus. Man was made from the dust of the ground. He was of the earth, earthy. He must be seen, first of all, as a part of the whole scheme of the animal creation. This means that he has the same fundamental impulses and instincts as the rest of the animal kingdom. With this view of man's physical development science is in substantial agreement, despite the fact that its theory of man's detailed development is stated differently. According to the Darwinian thesis, man was to be seen as a part of the whole scheme of the animal creation, which began with a few basic types from which all the others, including man, developed. Animal life, including man, represents a continuity. This is a genuine contribution to our understanding of man, for only as we see him in the light of his animal background can we understand some of the more objectionable traits of the genus Homo.

But this is only one side of the picture; man must be seen on the side of his spiritual nature. God "breathed into his nostrils the breath of life; and man became a living soul." Man is animal plus. He is a "living soul." Translated into modern language, this means man has the power of reason, the sense of responsibility, the instinct for the higher life. Here is to be found the basis for both the satisfactions and the disillusionments of man's life. It is these qualities which have made man the pioneer and the adventurer. They are the basis for his cultural life. They also explain his egoism and spirit of acquisitiveness, his desire for fame, his passion for power. All of these qualities are a part of mankind's mental and spiritual equipment which distinguish him from the lower animal life, and are the direct gift of God to him. The great need of our age is to have these God-given qualities brought under such controls as will make them a blessing to humanity rather than a curse.

3. *Man Has Supreme Worth and Dignity*

The one truth about man upon which all thinkers are agreed is the sacredness of human personality. According to the Scriptures, man was made in the image of God and had the possibility of becoming a son of God. In the estimation of Jesus men were of infinitely more value than the birds of the heavens or the lilies of the field. Our whole modern notion of democracy has its basis in the fundamental conviction of the worth of the ordinary man. Despite the fact that there are vast areas of life where this ideal has not yet been applied, and many groups of people who have had very little share in genuine democracy, there is a steadily growing determination that all men must ultimately share the good things of life provided by their heavenly Father. One is reminded, in this connection, of that familiar statement of Dr. Borden P. Bowne: "The individual may never be regarded as fuel for warming society. In a moral system, the good he produces, he must in some way share." [3]

One of the most devastating and most nearly unanswerable arguments against modern warfare, with its tremendous slaughter of the finest physical specimens of the young manhood in all the countries who are engaged in war, is the apparent lack of respect for the personalities of these young men. The day has long past when Christian democracy can regard them as "cannon fodder." Granted that there are causes of sufficient worth and merit to warrant such tremendous sacrifice of human life, these causes ought to be so manifest that he who runs may read them. Further, there ought to be the most resolute determination on the part of Christians of all lands that this brutal method of settling differences among men must end, and methods more in harmony with the spirit of Christ be developed.

4. *The Unity of Mankind*

One of the clearest emphases in both the Old and the New Testament is that of the unity of mankind. In the symbolic account in Genesis the whole human race is repre-

[3] *Principles of Ethics* (New York: American Book Company, 1909), p. 199.

sented as having descended from an original couple, Adam and Eve. As a result of the sin of these two, sin, suffering, and death became the lot of all mankind. Both Jesus and Paul were quite explicit in their expression of the fact of the solidarity of the human race. Time and again Jesus disregarded national and racial limitations in his statement of the all-inclusiveness of membership in the Kingdom of God. Paul insisted that God has made of one all the nations of men and that all men have the possibility of salvation, not because of their racial lineage, but through faith in Jesus Christ.

Much of the tragic bitterness and hatred now engulfing the world is due to the failure to appreciate the fact that the human race is one; that, according to Jesus, all people are members of one great family with God as Father, and all men are related to each other as brothers. As over against this ideal of Jesus, the situation in the world as we have it is race against race, nation against nation, class against class. The present World War is a dramatic testimony to the failure of mankind to accept the way of Christ in this area.

One of the genuine contributions of the present Nazi movement in Germany, whatever may have been the aims of the movement, has been the dramatization of this whole problem of race. They have demonstrated in unmistakable fashion what happens when a nation becomes "insane" on the race question. Perhaps never in the history of mankind has there been such persistent persecution and wholesale slaughter of innocent persons, for no other reason than their racial identity, as has been true in the case of members of the Jewish race located in the areas where the Nazi leaders are in control.

It is only fair, however, when we speak of the extremes of racial hatred to which the Nazi rulers in Germany have gone, that we remember this is just one of the "hot spots" in the world where the problem of race is manifest. It has become a problem of world-wide concern. Here in our own country we have one of the most difficult race problems to be found anywhere in the world. There are those who believe that the acid test of Christianity in the United States of America, if not in the world, will be our ability to find a Christian solution to our difficult problem of race. Incidentally, the strategic position which the United States will occupy following the war will give Christians in America a unique vantage point in the opportunity they will have to make a genuine contribution to the solution of this problem, if they themselves can make any substantial headway in this area of human relationships.

5. "All Men Are Sinners"

Both the Old and the New Testament seem to teach the universality of sin and an apparent native human bias toward evil. In Genesis 3 we have the story of the sin of the first man resulting in his "fall." In Romans 5:12-21 Paul, the great theologian of the early church, attributes the entrance of sin into the world to the transgression of the first man, Adam. It was Augustine, however, the greatest of the church fathers, who developed the doctrine of original sin as over against the actual sin committed by the individual. By original sin Augustine meant a fatal defect in man's nature which made it impossible for him not to sin. Even infants enter the world with this defect and are therefore inherently sinners before they have had a chance to commit any sins of their own.

While it seems clear that, for all practical purposes, all men are sinners and have fallen short of the will of God, modern man can no longer accept the notion of an original taint due to the act of the first man. Whatever of truth

59

there may be in the concept of "original sin" and its effect upon each person as he begins his life career would seem to be explained by his social inheritance and his background of nonmoral animal instincts and impulses. A typical definition given for sin is, "Sin is any want of conformity unto, or transgression of, the law of God." This implies conformity with moral standards and loyalty to God. Conformity with moral standards assumes a knowledge of what those standards are. No man can be held accountable for a moral obligation of which he is completely ignorant. The determination, therefore, of what is sin varies with different individuals.

In this connection the two factors alluded to above, the social inheritance and the nonmoral animal impulses, must be taken into account. There is the community or tribal code or mores which is frequently more exacting, and usually lower, than the individual code. Members of a community are expected to conform to the community code, irrespective of whether that code measures up to their own highest moral insights or not. Further, it frequently happens that, having had no opportunity for higher moral insights, individuals trained in the tribal code do not recognize their wrongdoing. Sin committed under those conditions could hardly be called sin, as far as the individual is concerned. It does, however, indicate the need for higher moral insights, since the evil results of such actions are just as real whether committed deliberately or in ignorance.

The other factor to be taken into account is that of the nonmoral animal instincts. Man the animal creature begins his work on the nonmoral plane with the same appetites, impulses, and instincts as the rest of the animal creation. These impulses, while not in themselves sinful, are quite active in the individual in those formative years before there has been developed in him the sense of moral values. It

60

is a short step from this situation to the yielding of the will which constitutes sin.

In the final analysis, the basis of sin is to be found in man's freedom and self-determination. That is the abiding significance of the story in Genesis. The essence of personality is freedom of choice. Not even God himself can prevent man's making wrong choices if he elects to do so. Nevertheless, these other factors of social inheritance and nonmoral instincts influence very greatly man's decisions. It is therefore encumbent upon each individual that he live up to his highest moral insights, seek constantly to raise the level of these insights, and always be loyal to what he believes to be the will of God. There would, finally, seem to be the need of a sense of corporate responsibility for raising the whole level of community ideals, so that growing individuals might have the social environment needed to develop the highest quality of Christian idealism.

6. *The Salvation of Mankind*

When the modern man faces the problem of "salvation," he realizes both his need of it and the source of it. "O wretched man that I am! who shall deliver me from the body of this death?" writes the great Apostle to the Gentiles in his Epistle to the Romans. It is this sense of sin, inescapable and ineradicable as far as his own efforts are concerned, which tends to make life a veritable prison house of the dead for all mankind. As the Apostle realizes, deliverance can come from only one source; that is God, through Jesus Christ. And so the Apostle writes: "For the law of the spirit of life in Christ Jesus hath made me free from the law of sin and death."

In these words the Apostle has symbolized the spiritual struggle that each individual faces as he seeks to free himself

61

from the law of sin and death. He finds in himself dispositions and attitudes out of harmony with his highest spiritual longings—those carnal desires and appetites which tend to debase him if allowed to control him. The early disciples of Jesus were a unit in their conviction that salvation was to come through Jesus Christ. In asserting the saviorhood of Jesus his followers were linking him to God as the means of salvation. Both in his life and death Jesus revealed the righteousness and love of God. What Christ did in his supreme act of self-sacrifice, God was doing. God was in Christ reconciling the world unto himself. Salvation was available to those who accepted Jesus as the revelation of God the Father and surrendered their wills to him.

Salvation, then, is the process by which man establishes a satisfactory relationship between himself and God, through the leadership of Jesus Christ. But the appeal to God and the sense of acceptance is only the beginning of the process. There must be growth unto the fullness of the stature of the man Christ Jesus. This is the essence of salvation—this continuous growth into the likeness of the man Christ Jesus. In outlining the conditions of salvation theologians have used such terms as "justification" and "sanctification." These terms, however, have little meaning to an age bred in ignorance of theological terminology. By justification they mean the process by which a man comes to the conviction that he has been pardoned of his sins and has been accepted by God as his loyal follower. Involved in the process is the recognition by man that he is in need of salvation from sin, that God the heavenly Father loves him despite the fact that he is a sinner and is willing to accept him as his child. When man makes the complete surrender of his will to God and has the sense of pardon for his sins, as well as the

THE CHRISTIAN CONCEPTION OF MAN

conviction that he has been accepted by God, he has achieved what the theologians called justification. Sanctification is the continuation of the process of Christlikeness. "It does not," as Dean Knudson reminds us, "denote perfection attained but progress toward it." [4] Here again the Apostle Paul has a word of wisdom for Christian pilgrims as given by Dr. Moffatt: "Brothers, I for one do not consider myself to have appropriated this; my one thought is, by forgetting what lies behind me and straining to what lies before me, to press on to the goal for the prize of God's high call in Christ Jesus."

All of this the modern man believes, but he senses difficulties which his medieval spiritual forebears did not feel. Salvation is not merely a matter of the individual's relation to God. It is also a matter of his relationship to the society of which he is a member, and the effect of his social environment upon him. In his book *Social Salvation* Dr. John C. Bennett has written most illuminatingly on this aspect of the problem of salvation. It is possible even to block the grace of God by allowing the unwholesome social conditions which deny to thousands of human beings, made in the image of God and capable of becoming sons of God, their chance for the abundant life which Christ came to give. For be it remembered that always with Christ his "abundant life" was a life that begins on earth here and now. It meant to proclaim release for captives, recovery of sight to the blind, giving freedom to the oppressed, preaching the good news to the poor. Any salvation worthy of the name Christian must be big enough to include both the individual and the community, and both earth and heaven in its scope.

[4] Albert C. Knudson, *The Doctrine of Redemption* (New York: Abingdon-Cokesbury Press, 1933), p. 411.

63

7. *Mankind Can Be Understood Only in the Light of Eternity*

Both the Old and the New Testament give evidence of man's dissatisfaction with his earth-bound limitations. This sense of dissatisfaction is first most completely and fully expressed in the Book of Job. It was clear to this author that life here was full of inequities. The innocent often suffered, while the wicked prospered. Surely there must be justice and fair play somewhere in the universe.

The author of the Book of Job finally came to the conviction that ultimately there would be vindication for the innocent sufferer. Jesus spoke frequently of the life eternal and the urgent need for trying to attain it. The point here is that the biblical writers were of the opinion that the life of a human being, made in the image of God, did not terminate with his physical disintegration. Mankind belonged to eternity. The hope of an abundant life beyond has been the mainspring of the Christian faith. What may the modern thinker believe about man's ultimate destiny in the light of the new world picture?

In the first place, the fact must be frankly faced that in recent years a marked skeptical tendency has developed relative to belief in the life after death. Some of the reasons for this, as Dean Knudson reminds us, may be found in: (*a*) the utter insignificance of the creature man as compared with the vastness of the physical universe; (*b*) the dependence of the mind on the body; (*c*) the new social interest, where the emphasis on the place and prerogatives of the individual has been subordinated to the emphasis on the society of which he is a member; (*d*) our absorption in the interests of the physical world, the knowledge of which has become so much greater that we do not seem to need this interest in another world. And finally, may it not be found in the growth of a practical materialism produced by our machine age which brings us a greater degree of comfort and prosperity in this world than man has ever experienced?

As man, however, comes face to face with death, the last and greatest enemy of the race, he has had to face the question of its relation to human destiny; for, as Berdyaev reminds us, "Death is the most profound and significant fact in the world." It is the fact of death which gives real meaning to the question of life. The most faithful interpreters of the life and death of Jesus have insisted that in both of these experiences, life and death, he gave the most significant answer. Through Christ "death is swallowed up in victory. O death, where is thy sting? O grave, where is thy victory?" In Christ's resurrection from the dead we seem to have the answer. That has been the faith of the church all through the centuries, and in this faith it has triumphed.

And what is the rational basis for this faith? The two types of arguments which have seemed most satisfactory in this connection are the ethical and the religious. In the case of the ethical argument, as Dean Knudson suggests, the reasoning has developed in two different directions: the need of the future life to redress the wrongs of the present life; and the moral incompleteness of the present life, the need of another world theater in which to develop the life so imperfectly lived here. In the first emphasis just ordinary fair play and elemental justice seem to demand that good people who have suffered inequities in this life be, somewhere, given a chance to live their lives in a more healthy moral environment. A just God would seem to be obligated, ultimately, to make this possible. In the second place, man has a sense of frustration, even when he has done his best, when he places his own moral achievements up against those demanded by the good God, as illustrated in the life of his best exemplar in the world, Jesus Christ. He needs a more friendly moral climate in which to achieve such moral perfection.

The religious argument takes into account both the nature of God and the nature of man. Men seem instinctively to long for immortality. This would seem to argue for the validity of the conception. While this fact is not in itself conclusive proof of immortality, it helps to support the belief when added to more convincing data. The final and most convincing proof of the life after death would seem to be found in the nature of God himself, as revealed in Jesus Christ. Said Jesus in that great passage which was his answer to the heart hunger of mankind through the years: "Ye believe in God, believe also in me. . . . . I go to prepare a place for you. And if I go and prepare a place for you, I will come again, and receive you unto myself; that where I am, there ye may be also." That is to say, God's nature demands that another world theater be prepared for the restless and eternal spirit of man; and faith in God, as revealed in Jesus Christ, is the assurance of the fact that such a provision has been made.

Finally, the only justification for the manifestly high view of man so evident in the cultural, moral, and spiritual qualities that distinguish him from the lower animal life would seem to be found in his destiny for the higher life, a life hid with Christ in God. About the details of that life we may well be modest. It is enough to be able to say with another great soul who lived much closer to the beginnings of the Christian faith: "And it doth not yet appear what we shall be: but we know that, when he shall appear, we shall be like him; for we shall see him as he is."

A CHRISTIAN VIEW OF NATURE

Edgar S. Brightman
Professor of Philosophy, Boston University

Nature is the permanent setting for human history in this stage of the universe. Prewar, postwar, and war, Nature is always with us. This chapter proposes to set forth a Christian philosophy of Nature—Christian in the sense that it is consistent with the values taught by Christ. Nature will be taken to mean the world of matter and energy investigated by the sciences of physics, chemistry, and biology, that is, the world of things moving in space. It is taken for granted that consciousness (mind, personality) is not matter or physical energy, and that psychology, in so far as it deals with mind, is not a natural science.

A Christian philosophy of Nature will consist neither of romantic ecstasies nor of cold indifference to Nature. Jesus wisely counseled us to consider the lilies, not to gasp at them nor to ignore them. Following his clue, this chapter will aim at a reasoned definition of Nature and of the relations of Nature to God and to the Christian way of life.

Almost every vital religious and social movement in the world rests on a philosophy of Nature. Naziism, Nipponism, Communism, Roman Catholicism, Calvinism, and Christian Science are all vital, and all draw a large part of their power from action based on a clear-cut philosophy of Nature which is accepted—if not understood—by every loyal member of the rank and file. The average Protestant—be it noted that Calvinists are not average—is the only religious believer in the world who tries to get on in complete ignorance of any philosophy of Nature. When we add that Protestantism is in the doldrums, it is not to assert that the doldrums are wholly due to the ignorance. Yet the drift to the doldrums is in part a direct result of the ignorance and confusion of our minds. Confusion? Yes, but the real trouble lies not so much in tempestuous winds of doctrine as in a deadly intellectual calm, a smug indifference to thought. There is no great and continuous spiritual power without great thought. Weak and flabby thinking yields weak and flabby living. To quote the "good Bishop Berkeley": "Whatever the world thinks, he who hath not much meditated upon God, the human mind, and the *summum bonum,* may possibly make a thriving earthworm, but will most indubitably make a sorry patriot and a sorry citizen." [1] In approaching thought about God through thought about Nature we are following Berkeley's example.

I. POSSIBLE VIEWS OF NATURE

There are, of course, views of Nature that are hostile to any Christian belief. For example, Nature may be taken to be a scene of ruthlessness that justifies man in boundless egoism or pessimism or both. "Nature, red in tooth and claw with ravine, shrieks," and man shrieks too. Again, the facts of race and heredity may be taken as a natural basis for racial pride and aggression. When the blood and soil of one nation are exalted as Nature's choicest product, the unfailing destiny of Germany or of Japan—or even of God's country—is guaranteed. Hitler's view of himself

[1] *Siris,* sec. 350.

as "the instrument of the Creator of the Universe" is more than matched by the ancient Shinto faith [2] in the emperor of Nippon as "God incarnate" and in the Japanese nation as "co-eternal with heaven and earth."

Then there are views of Nature indifferent to Christian values. Many naturalists and neorealists take the position that Nature is neutral to all values. This view is quite compatible with Christian ethics, but not with faith in a Heavenly Father.

A positively Christian view is one that finds in Nature the presence of God. Such a view will be defined in this chapter. "He maketh his sun to rise on the evil and on the good." The view that will be presented is not offered as the only Christian one, nor is any attempt made to prove it here. It will be enough to define consistently the faith that God is actually present in Nature.

Before proceeding to this central task, it is well to warn the reader of the differences among philosophers. Some hold to impersonal naturalism and find in Nature no trace of a God; some accept dualism and believe that God creates or works through an unspiritual and purely material substance; some are pantheists and identify God with the universe. The definitions of this chapter, however, will start from personalism as a working hypothesis. Personalism is the belief that the universe is a society of persons and that Nature consists of personal consciousness and of nothing else. Some personalists think that Nature is a system of many tiny selves or persons, which they call monads or cells, governed by God; others find in Nature the presence and power of one person only, namely, God. The differences are technical and need not detain us here. Those

[2] See Genchi Kato, *A Study of Shinto, the Religion of the Japanese Nation* (Tokyo: Meiji Japan Society, 1926), pp. 49, 203, etc.

who hold the first view (panpsychists) and those who hold the second one (immanentists) agree that Nature is personal, that God governs it, and that human persons are a society related to God but no part of him.[3] This chapter will approach the problem from the immanentist standpoint held by Berkeley, Lotze, Bowne, and many others, according to which physical Nature is divine consciousness and physical energy is divine will in action under the conditions which the divine experience fixes. As Berkeley put it, the things of Nature are a "language of the Author of Nature." The psalmist's dictum that "the heavens declare the glory of God" is philosophically sound, on the basis of the hypothesis of personalism, which we are now going to try for what it is worth.

II. God as Transcendent to Nature

The gods of ancient religions have for the most part been transcendent beings. They have not been present in Nature, or if they were, they were restricted to tree or river or some other local habitat. Most of the old gods dwelt far away, on Mount Olympus or in some distant heaven; only occasionally did they come into the natural order in response to man's call or on some special errand of their own. The Hebrew couldn't "sing the Lord's song in a strange land." God lived in Jerusalem, or "between the cherubim," which was inconvenient when a person happened to be in Babylonian exile. The thought of God's omnipresence dawned slowly.

Why is God thought of as far away before he is seen to be near by? For one thing, God is hard to find, anyway. For another, the ordinary course of Nature does not seem to be friendly or adorable. Besides, values reside

---

[3] Charles Hartshorne, however, is a panpsychist who views persons as parts of God.

in the soul, not in mere things; primitive man did not need to wait for a German philosopher to come along and intone the syllables *wertfrei* (free from value) before he realized that spiritual life needs more than appears on the surface of the stocks and stones of Nature.

Nature has value only in relation to personality. Much of Nature seems not to feed or delight or exalt or protect the soul. The ordinary course of Nature seems either indifferent or hostile; God is not visibly there. Only when Nature is friendly is God at hand. When men became more thoughtful, they saw that their own ideal life transcended their sensations. As values, purposes, and love are transcendent to sensations, so, they reasoned, divine values, divine purposes, divine love, are transcendent to Nature. Socrates in the *Phaedo* explained that he sat in prison not because his flesh and bones brought him there, but because he chose to obey the laws of Athens; Nature would run away and escape, but grace held him to his ideals.

Thus God is more than Nature, and, in an important sense, other than Nature. Regardless of technical definitions and labels, there is more in the universe than all that is investigated by the sciences of matter and motion. The "more" is the key to the divine. Without plans, ideals, and reasons that are "more" than motion, Nature could never be known nor used. Knowledge of Nature implies a knower that is not Nature, values that are not Nature. Nature presupposes the transcendent and the supernatural; but the supernatural is disclosed in value experience and personal unity far more clearly than in what has traditionally been regarded as the miraculous. The transcendent God of love is revealed in all signs of rational purpose rather than in deviations from rational purpose. The ancient problem of miracle has distracted attention from the main point. The transcendent transcends sense experience; it does not transcend all experience.

If we mortals have transcendent experiences—experiences transcending the data of sense—and if God is transcendent, then God can never be adequately known through the most adequate knowledge of Nature. Nature is indeed a clue to God. Enlarging knowledge of Nature enlarges our thought of God. Copernicus and Darwin, Jeans and Eddington, have given us a greater conception of God by giving us a greater conception of Nature. Nevertheless, God is more than all possible Nature. No space can contain his unbegun and unending purposes of inexhaustible love and beauty and growth, or the eternal unity of his creative personality, or his knowledge. We learn more important truths about God from the history and development of man's spiritual life than we do from any knowledge of Nature.

To say this is not at all to disparage science. On the contrary, it is fully to accept science for what it is, namely, a partial description of the changes that occur in Nature. On our hypothesis, this means that science is a partial description of God's verifiable behavior. It is, however, far more in harmony with the spirit of science to recognize the specialized and abstract character of scientific knowledge than it would be to see in science a revelation of God's full being and purpose. Every science is abstract, that is, selective; physics and chemistry, which define the limits of Nature, deliberately and necessarily omit all investigation of personality and its values (once the value of scientific investigation is granted—and forgotten). On the other hand, it is absurd to infer from this that science is irrelevant to religion. Religion and science are attitudes of one human mind toward one and the same universe. They must, therefore, be related both subjectively and objectively. If science does not disclose the supernatural and redemptive purposes of God, it nevertheless discloses all we know about the means and powers used by God on the natural level. The laws of science are the ways of working of the God of Nature. They are what Bowne used to call the supernatural natural. We therefore turn to a consideration of immanence.

III. Nature as Immanent in God

It is usually said that God is immanent in Nature. This statement, however, involves a lurking presupposition that Nature is really external to God, and that God somehow enters into it and dwells there. To get away from all such picture-thinking, let us frankly posit that Nature is wholly within God.

If Nature is within God, as less than his entire being, then we presuppose that God transcends Nature. True as this is, the truth has often been exaggerated to the point of caricature. On the one hand, Nature has been made a second God, so independent as to crowd out the first and real God. On the other hand, God has been pictured as so remote from Nature that one could hardly speak even of remote control. An "absentee" God is hardly one of whom the heart—or head—grows fonder. Recent theology has been so eager to exalt God above Nature that it has sometimes put him entirely out of reach. The transcendent Being of the Barthians has concerned himself directly with Nature but rarely; since the week of creation, perhaps only in the first century of the Christian era. This single intervention over, he veiled himself in distant clouds—supernatural ones, not natural. Such a view makes creation a magic miracle, vitiates the evidence for God in Nature, and renders any relation between personality and Nature unintelligible. We should, it is true, humbly accept all real mystery in "this mysterious Universe." But that duty of humility is far from obligating us to "throw a dust in the air and then complain we cannot see," to quote the good Berkeley again.

The insight which has commonly been called the theory of the immanence of God in Nature is intended to dispel this dust. If Nature be something other than God—as dualists suppose—in which God comes to dwell, then one may rightly speak of God's immanence in Nature. But if Nature be what the personalistic hypothesis supposes, then it is, as was previously said, far truer to think of Nature as immanent in God. Let us now examine further the idea that Nature is an organization of the divine consciousness, and so, literally speaking, an integral part of the divine personality.

Personalistic immanentism is a monistic view of Nature. Nature manifests one controlling power, not two or more. The idea that God controls Nature in so far as it is favorable to man and that Satan takes over when tempest or disease rages is naïve. It implies a sort of gentleman's agreement between God and the devil to conform to the same laws and to co-operate perfectly so far as Nature is concerned. This is derogatory to the supposed character of both parties to the agreement. There is one set of laws, one table of elements, one mathematics, one interactive system, revealed in the entire astrophysical universe. It doubtless is true that many wills avail themselves of the laws of the system of Nature and that it operates, as Jesus taught, with its sun and its rains, for the uses of both evil and good, both just and unjust. But the system is one, and exhibits a unitary source—whether we call that source the Demiurge of Plato, the Absolute of Hegel, or the Father of our Lord Jesus Christ, who taught that birds and human beings are fed by the same Father, and that the beauty of lilies and the clothing of man are alike God's work.

The considerations which point to a unitary, rational being in Nature are supplemented by further arguments against any kind of metaphysical dualism or "bifurcation." "The bifurcation of Nature" was a phrase perhaps suggested to Whitehead's mind by the bifurcation of the River Stour that creates the island of Thanet on which he was born. Whatever the origin of the phrase, any bifurcation of Nature that divides it into kinds of being that have no powers or properties in common is a sheer mystification that makes science impossible and philosophy dogmatic. It is true that what we inanely call "common sense" tells us that we see matter to be something utterly different from mind in all respects. It is also true that the world of Nature is actually the work of a superhuman energy indescribably greater than human mind. But it is not true that these considerations prove dualism to be a correct description of the differences between Nature and human mind. Far from being correct, dualism is incoherent and unempirical. It is incoherent because it renders any relation or interaction between the two realms so contradictory to the defined properties of matter and mind as to require more than a Cartesian pineal gland to overcome the conflict. It is unempirical because all the empirical evidence we have for Nature is found in the form of consciousness, which indicates that Nature throughout its being is at least related to consciousness, able to appear in it, and harmonious with its conditions. From these facts it is reasonable to infer that Nature and personality are constituted of one and the same kind of stuff, the stuff of personality. Personality is sufficiently complex to contain all the diverse qualities and powers revealed in Nature, but it also is an indivisible but complex unity.

Thus far it has been shown that dualism will not suffice

75

—whether a dualism of God and Satan or of matter and mind. Whatever variety there is in Nature must be within, and coherent with, the fundamental unity of the eternal Person. There is, however, a protest against monism and immanentism from the panpsychists. Panpsychism, already mentioned, has been increasingly popular since Leibnitz. It is the view that Nature is not the experience of one great mind, but is rather the interaction of countless small selves or monads, somehow under God's guidance —as most panpsychists believe. This view does away with the nonsense of dualism, and takes due account of the empirical fact of consciousness. It seems also to be in harmony with scientific analysis of life into cells and of inorganic matter into atoms and of them into protons, electrons, neutrons. For each element there is a monad. But these empirical advantages are counteracted by the incoherence of the theory. We have to explain both the variety and the harmony of the order of Nature. Panpsychism does very well with the variety but very poorly with the harmony. How can the panpsychist ascribe to each monad sufficient power and intelligence to be aware of all the laws of Nature and to conform to them? What is the use of supposing so many monads in a uniform order? Or if, as recent scientists are coming to believe, the order is not absolutely uniform, how could independent, free, and rebellious monads be made to approximate as much agreement as we find in Nature? The order of Nature requires one purpose, one plan, one mind. The more the monads are used to explain deviations from absolute uniformity the less they can be used to explain Nature's unity. They are, if anything ever was, entities multiplied beyond necessity. They clutter the universe up; they raise dust.

One might pause to ask why thinkers have been so eager to avoid seeing God in Nature. Why did Philo require a

76

Logos to deal with Nature, rather than having God to do so directly? Why did Neoplatonists make God so remote? Why all these dualisms, these many monads, where God belongs? One motive, at least, is to preserve the exalted dignity of God; if he is viewed as a divine Aristocrat, then he will not be expected to soil his hands with labor in Nature. Professor J. B. Pratt does not like a "very busy God" who regulates every motion of every electron and proton within his experience. A God so great as the immanent One, so near and so vast at once, is almost too terrifyingly great for the ordinary imagination to grasp; and so men push God out of Nature so as to see him in a sort of perspective. Then, when they think Nature can get along without him, they gradually come to think either that they can get along without him if Nature can, or else that they can reach him only by a supernatural and even unnatural revelation. Either alternative is a profound religious and intellectual loss.

In so far as these dualisms and panpsychisms dwell on the complexity of Nature, they are pointing toward truth. The variety of Nature is obvious. In life, as Darwin says at the end of *The Origin of Species*, "endless forms most beautiful and most wonderful have been, and are being evolved." In Nature there are law and chance, mathematics and incalculable qualities, inexhaustible combinations. But all this variety is no evidence against the presence of all Nature within the unifying personality of God. Rather it betokens need of a unifying principle. As William Stern pointed out, the essence of a person is to be a complex unity (*unitas multiplex*). Only unrelated variety or undifferentiated unity would be incompatible with personality. Personality includes and unifies variety.

Nature, on this immanentist hypothesis, is in God. All of Nature is God's experience. Every event in Nature involves God's will, as well as whatever there is in God that is not will—what Schelling called *"der göttliche Unwille."* Yet this emphasis on the immanence of Nature in God should not cause us to forget that Nature is one realm in a divine mind of many realms. God is far more, far greater, than all of Nature. Whether the law of entropy will result in the running down of all the physical universe, or cosmic radiation is inexhaustible and Nature will never cease to be, is a question unanswered by science, by philosophy, and by religion. Its answer is of far greater importance to science than to philosophy or religion. Whether Nature is an episode in the divine history or a permanent, but subordinate phase of it, is not a vital question. What is vital is that Nature is much less than the whole of God; his reason, his love, his beauty, his moral and social purpose transcend Nature far more than human loyalty transcends any act of physical courage or than true human love transcends any deed that expresses it. Yet Nature and the supernatural reason and purpose of God are integral to one and the same mind, as sensation, thought, and purpose are integral to the mind of man.

On this view, Nature is a divine language. Every event in Nature is a revelation of God. This is the faith of idealists everywhere—in India, in Germany, in Britain, in America. To quote Dr. Frederick de W. Bolman's recent translation of Schelling's *The Ages of the World*: "The whole spatially extended universe is nothing but the swelling heart of the godhead. Held by invisible powers, it persists in a continual pulsation, or alternation of expansion and contraction." [4]

This monistic immanentism may confuse those who fail to recall clearly the definition of Nature as the realm

[4] (New York: Columbia University Press, 1942), p. 215.

78

of physics to be distinguished from the realm of psychology. Naturalists, if they recall this definition, will doubtless object to it. They will call it too narrow. How absurd, they would say, to exclude man from Nature, or to divide man and assign his body to Nature and his soul to a different order. They, the naturalists, are not talking about any such Nature as was defined. Nature, for them, includes man, his evolution, his kinship with the world, and his ideal aspirations.

At this point it is easy to fall into a barren dispute about words. The real question is not whether we should use a broader or a narrower meaning for the word Nature. The real question is whether categories derived from the narrower meaning shall be used to restrict and even to negate categories revealed by the broader meaning. If the word experience (instead of Nature) be employed to mean the whole field of consciousness with all its content and its affirmations, then we can and must distinguish between our experiences of objects believed to be located in physical space and our experiences of personal and social values, ideals, and loyalties. If the naturalist is arguing that all of these types of experience must be accepted as somehow belonging together in one world, one common order, in which there is no ultimate bifurcation, then the naturalist and the personal idealist are so far saying the same thing. But if the naturalist adds, as he usually does, that the physical order of experiences shows us what Nature objectively is, and that there is nothing objectively real except Nature, he is engaged in an unempirical reductionism. He reduces spirit to matter. He forgets all his pleas for including values and ideals in Nature when he comes to defining what Nature is. The personal idealist, who takes our senses as revealing one aspect of the real and our ideal values as revealing another and far more important aspect, is both more inclusive and more connected in his thinking than is the naturalist. All our evidence for every belief we have is the evidence of consciousness; impersonal naturalism provides a very inadequate account of that evidence.

Every view of Nature, and of matter, society, or God, must start with the fact of personal consciousness, not merely because the evidence is located there, but also because it is all we have and are in our immediate existence. Personal consciousness is the situation we directly experience; Nature is a system of situations we believe in. Our belief in Nature is well grounded, but it is grounded only in our personal consciousness. All appeals to social or public verification serve but to conceal the fact that our belief in the existence of society itself is derived solely from evidence found in our individual personalities.

What, then, is a person? From the strictly empirical standpoint a person is a unity of complex present conscious experience, connected with past and future experiences by self-identifying memories and anticipations, and gifted with the power to think and to achieve ideal values. The unity and self-identity of a person are evidence of his privacy. "The monads have no windows," in the sense that no one else can experience me or be my self, although I am in constant interaction with God, and with all other persons in my environment. Persons are at once private and interactive, unique and social, dependent and free.

The hypothesis of personalism is that the universe is a society of persons—or of selves, including both subpersonal, human, and superhuman selves. God, who includes all Nature, is the greatest person; but all persons form a society dependent on God for their existence, interacting with him and with each other through him, yet in no sense identical with him. The whole society is a communicating, interacting society. Degrees of interaction and modes of communication vary. Nature may be viewed, quasi-pantheistically, as part of God, but persons are companions of God—friendly, ignorant, or hostile. To view Nature as part of God is compatible with all the facts and relates their variety and their unity in the complex unity of God's personality. But human persons—and such other persons as there may be—cannot be regarded as parts of God's mind without contradiction. Human beings indubitably experience ignorance, error, and sin; and to ascribe their experiences to God, so that they exist in him exactly as they exist in us, is to make God's mind a congeries of ignorance and incoherence. Personality is private, and no person is a part of any other person, even of God, although all persons depend on and interact with God, certainly through Nature and often through other spiritual means of communication from soul to soul—"the flight of the Alone to the Alone."

This social personalism combines the merits and avoids the defects of both pantheism and dualism, of naturalism and of supernaturalism. It should be repeated, in distinguishing immanentist personalism from pantheism, that the immanence of God in persons is very different from the immanence of Nature in God. There is, according to immanentist personalism, nothing in Nature that is not in God as a veritable part of his personal consciousness. But God's immanence in persons other than himself precludes the idea that any other person is a part of God. God's immanence in other persons, then, means that he wills them to exist as other than himself, yet dependent on him and constantly interacting with him. By his continuous activity he gives them data of experience, which constitute their field of choice; and he also gives them

81

the power of self-determining freedom, freedom always within limits, yet always able to say "yes" or "no" to any alternative which experience presents. The goal of this freedom, God's kingdom, is a society of free co-operators.

IV. Nature and Christian Life

In Nature man's life in wartime is being lived, and in Nature it will be lived after the war. Nature has now been defined to be the very life and being of God in one area of his personality. If natural life is seen to be life in God, new light is shed on many aspects of Christian living. Let us offer a few hints.

There is, for example, a new view of the relation between Nature and sin. The old theology has taken Nature as being under a curse, and heredity as being the transmission of original sin. If Nature is God in action, it cannot be under a curse. Nature is not sinful either originally or derivatively. Adam's sin was Adam's and not ours, unless we imitate it. Natural desires and acts are not inherently evil; man alone creates the curse and the sin when he misuses God's Nature.

Nature, however, is a source of both sufferings and joys; that is, God is their source. Traditional Christianity has sometimes exalted the sufferings as blessings and disparaged the joys as temptations. But if Nature is immanent in God, then God is a fellow sufferer of the evils and a fellow rejoicer in the joys that Nature offers. As integral to God, suffering becomes meaningful and true joy becomes eternal. The Lamb slain from the foundation of the world will reign forever and ever. If there is Calvary in God, there is also Easter.

The view of this chapter also sheds new light on worship. It does not encourage Nature worship; to worship a part of God instead of his whole being is idolatry. Cow

82

worship is not Christian or philosophical. But immanent-ism does give us what A. A. Bowman has called—in a slightly different connection—"a sacramental universe." It suggests that the worshiper may see in every natural fact the actual presence of God, as the Catholic worshiper sees God in the elements of the Holy Communion. What is required, then, is not some mystic miracle to transubstantiate Nature. Nature is already the very body of our Lord. What needs transubstantiation is the blind intellect and the sinful will of man. When man sees God in Nature, contemplates and adores him, and wills to co-operate with him, then the true sacrament of mystical worship is consummated. The miracle is one of will and insight, not one of magic.

Perhaps the most important, and certainly the most practical, consequence of the immanentist view is its interpretation of human welfare. It is, of course, possible to be devoted to human values while regarding Nature as neutral or even as hostile to those values. If, however, a co-operative response from Nature's God is reasonable to expect and possible to find experimentally, it is most unwise not to try the experiment. Simple everyday experience shows that, within limits, Nature does respond to human efforts. The soil yields harvests, children are born, beauty appears in life. All this happens just as if Nature were working with us and for us, although never for us alone. Moreover, Nature, that is, Nature's God, bestows the highest of enduring joys on those who live for righteous love in the world. Devotion to justice and co-operation among men and women of all races and creeds produces the happiest life known to man. God responds with generous gifts of joy even to those who deny or misunderstand him. Do we not all misunderstand him—although in varying degrees? Yet does not every sincere soul find him—again, in varying degrees?

We can, it is true, survive without relating our ideals of human welfare to an eternal personal spirit in Nature. If anyone is interested in minimum living, he will be satisfied to survive without conscious experience of God. We can live without it; God will see to that. But if ever there was a time in world history when minimum belief and minimum strength and minimum values were an unworthy aim in life, now is that time. For the individual, life can be lived very comfortably without knowledge of science, or of classical music, or of the church, or of friends outside the domestic circle; it can be lived much more comfortably without knowledge of man's fiendish inhumanity to man, or of God's justice. He who desires comfortable minimum living had best be warned: Beware of God! Keep away from the enlarging faith, the abundant life, the new powers, new tasks, new duties, that arise when one sees God in Nature, and Nature in God. Life that sees God has to change. It has to abandon racial prides and hates, the pride of economic privilege, of social station and of personal endowments. The utmost endeavors of an all-out war effort are but sounding brass and tinkling cymbals in comparison with what humanity would achieve if once it really saw God's presence in Nature, and availed itself of God's dangerous friendship. Friendship, yes; and dangerous too, dangerous to everything selfish, cruel, and war-making among men.

A Christian view of Nature sees in Nature the God revealed who gives dignity to man as his child, who gives substance to the hope of inexhaustible growth in the future, who gives strength and calm through his mystical friendship, and who rescues us from the hopelessness of materialism. The postwar world must experiment. Let it experiment with God.

84

THE SPIRITUAL BASIS OF DEMOCRACY[1]

UMPHREY LEE

President, Southern Methodist University
Dallas, Texas

To those who remember the careless gestures with which so many writers of books and articles in the twenties and thirties dismissed religion, it should be very heartening to hear the loud cheers for religion and democracy now rising from the Right benches, with even occasional, if somewhat weak, "bravos" from the Left wing. It *should* be encouraging, I say; and it would be if the intelligent Christian could think that these recent converts know what they are talking about. They remind one a little of Arnobius, the Latin apologist, who was converted at sixty and immediately wrote a vigorous defense of Christianity, although ignorant both of the Bible and of Christian doctrine. All of us welcome the growing recognition of the role of religion in democratic life, but we feel the need for a little more clarity in discussion.

Definitions are admittedly not fashionable, and one hesitates to begin by trying to define. But some people, reasonably or not, when they are invited to a discussion prefer to know what is being discussed. And those who think this academic fussiness forget that, if one cannot al-

[1] Some of the material in this lecture was used in an address to the Southern Association of Colleges and Secondary Schools in 1942, and was published in the *Southern Association Quarterly*. It is used here by permission.

ways settle the question by defining some disputed term, he can at least say what he means and try to mean the same thing for fifteen minutes. It will be necessary, then, to explain what is meant—in this paper—by democracy. One hears so much of democratic ways of life and democratic processes and democratic goals that one is pardonably confused. Most misleading of all is the use of the word "democracy" as the name of the vague goal toward which humanity is supposed to be moving in family, in church, in school, and everywhere else. It is certainly not helpful to treat democracy as if it were the sum of all our desiring. We yet "praise God from whom all blessings flow," and for a time it may be better to regard democracy as something less than the *summum bonum.*

I am not suggesting to you that anyone can define democracy satisfactorily. As Laski put it, "Men have found its essence in the character of the electorate, the relation between government and the people, the absence of wide economic differences between citizens, the refusal to recognize privileges built on birth or wealth, race or creed." [2] It would be helpful, however, if we adopted a definition, and there seems to be none better than that implied by Lincoln: "government of the people, by the people, for the people." If it is objected that this is defining democracy in political terms, it can be replied that this is what both the friends and enemies of democracy are talking about at the present moment.

Several speeches could be made against this type of definition. But before they are made, I should like to point out that no one doubts that economic and social questions are involved in discussions of democracy; but the crucial question is: Do we expect to use political means to achieve

[2] Harold J. Laski, art. "Democracy," *Encyclopaedia of the Social Sciences* (New York: The Macmillan Co., 1937).

the democratic life? If we propose using only persuasion, education, and candy bars, then we can forget about politics. But if, on the other hand, we intend to have laws passed and enforced, we are dealing with political problems. There may come a time when the anarchist's dream will come true; but until many years after those of us here have gone wherever we are going, social reforms will be finally achieved only when they are written into the statute books and enforced by the courts and the police. Surely no one expects that such far-reaching changes in our economic system as some advocate, or even the moderate changes which are more widely accepted, can be made by merely saying, "Naughty, naughty!" to the economic aggressors. In spite of all the talk about social and economic democracy, we must be interested primarily in political democracy. If it is true that we cannot have political democracy until we have social democracy, it is nevertheless true that our aim as a nation, a political unit, is the achievement of our social goals by political processes.

What is implied in Abraham Lincoln's words? It has long been a political theory that power is of the people. This is not peculiar to democracy; the Fascist nations claim that their government is of the people. But government *by* the people means that the people operate, direct, this government; and this goes a great deal further. Under this definition one cannot have a benevolent autocracy, not even an aristocracy of good people. "For the people" means that the object of government is the welfare of the citizens. But one must add that this is to be interpreted as Lincoln himself would have interpreted it, that it means without regard to race or religion and that it means the people individually.

Our problem, in so far as democracy may be achieved in organized society, is concrete. How can the people decide what is best for them? How can they translate their decision into actuality? And this, as we all know well enough, involves a multitude of matters. Economic and social factors must be reckoned with at every step of the way. There are problems of mental development and, as we shall see later, of moral maturity.

Yet the glory—and the tragedy—of democracy is that the people must decide their own course. True, there are all sorts of obstacles to their making a choice and to their expression of it. But the obstacles must be removed, and the people must make the choices. No short cut is possible. No specious talk about this or that being the way people would take if they had a chance to understand the matter, no argument that this is best for them, can serve as an excuse for totalitarian methods. Only when we are fighting for our lives do we dare to act without regard to the popular will expressed in some ordered fashion. Let us be very clear about this, for it is easy to repeat meaningless words about the whole matter. No one supposes that we today, in America or anywhere else, have a clear expression of the people's will. There are all sorts of obstacles—propaganda, election laws, party chicanery, and all the rest. Nobody supposes, further, or should suppose, that if we had the clear expression of the people's will it would necessarily be right or well-informed. But one must not make this an excuse for asserting that we can have a democratic government—we should now say rather a political life in a far wider sense than was dreamed of in Lincoln's day—"for the people" except as we have it "by the people." And this is what amuses our enemies and discourages our friends.

But we are to discuss the spiritual basis of democracy. Again we must define: "spiritual" may mean anything or nothing. I take it that we really are to talk about what

88

basis for democracy may be found in the Christian religion, or at most the Jewish-Christian religious tradition. Personally I shall be much more at home if I talk about the one religion with which I have some passing acquaintance. If this is not what I am meant to discuss, you will at least be under no misapprehension as to what I think I am talking about.

Some statements should be made at the beginning. In the first place, all Christians are not democrats, not even in the sense in which my father might have subscribed to that statement. As a matter of fact, there have been religious people, even religious people in the tradition of Western Christianity, who have lived under the Caesars or under the czars and have not believed it necessary to find another form of government. There are, moreover, Christians today who subscribe to the political doctrines of either the Communists or the Nazis, as can easily be seen by perusing the writings of the Dean of Canterbury and of Friedrich Gogarten. If one talks about democracy and religion, therefore, one must be specific as to the religion one means and as to the interpreters of that religion whom one approves.

In the second place, it should be understood that certain characteristics of the historic religion which all of us in the West inherit in some form are at variance with what some people understand as democratic processes. One may as well start with a paragraph from John Dewey's book *Freedom and Culture*. In his stimulating chapter on "Democracy and Human Nature" Dewey writes:

The real trouble is that there is an intrinsic split in our habitual attitudes when we profess to depend upon discussion and persuasion in politics and then systematically depend upon other methods in reaching conclusions in matters of morals and religion, or in anything where we depend upon a person

89

or group possessed of "authority." We do not have to go to theological matters to find examples. In homes and in schools, the places where the essentials of character are supposed to be formed, the usual procedure is settlement of issues, intellectual and moral, by appeal to the "authority" of parent, teacher, or textbook.[3]

Dewey asserts that this procedure is likely to result in the development of antidemocratic attitudes, for it is the use of antidemocratic ways to achieve democratic ends.

Now we shall agree, to save argument, that no one advocates the "father-is-right" or the "thus-saith-the-book" way of teaching either morals or arithmetic; but the cleavage in thought goes deeper than this. I am doing no injury to one of the greatest of American thinkers when I point out that what is really involved is not technique but the existence of any ultimate authority, even that sanctioning the dictum that there *should* be the possibility of the "release, maturing, and fruition of potentialities of human nature," which is, I believe, an essential of democracy as Professor Dewey understands it.

I am not at the moment arguing the truth or falsity of the position that nowhere must one accept any final authority. And certainly I am not capable of passing upon the pedagogical controversy as to whether children should ever accept statements upon authority. I admit that I have had my trust in certain modern methods sadly shaken. I have seen my own child much perplexed because he had been taught that he was to pursue the truth together with his teacher, but when he came to the end of the pursuit, he found that the answer was in the back of the book and that no amount of further pursuit of the truth and no ingenuity in that pursuit would permit him to arrive at any

[3] New York: G. P. Putnam's Sons, 1939.

other solution. Whether he would have been equally troubled if he had been told in the first place that there was only one answer and that had been determined before he was born, I do not know. Such mysteries are too deep for me.

Concerning such religion as we have inherited in this Western world I may speak with more confidence. In our religion there is an authority which cannot be done away. If, therefore, to serve democracy, first principles of all kinds and in all fields must be arrived at without any consideration of a Divinely Given, the historical religion of the Western world might as well be left out of account—as indeed it has been by many. There have, it is true, been attempts to "democratize theology." Bishop Francis J. McConnell records the statement of the gentleman who, having listened carefully to an uncompromising exposition of Calvinistic predestination, announced that God might foreordain people in the East to everlasting punishment, but the folks in Arkansas wouldn't stand for it. At the present time the most conservative would admit that moral codes are in large part socially determined, and that there is no little relativity in moral ideas. On the other hand, most liberals would now hold that there is moral finality. Like Chesterson, they believe that if you are going to do away with right and wrong you might also dispense with right and left. In short, it can now be said of most American Christians that both conservatives and liberals agree that some moral principles are ultimates—as, for instance, the principle that this world is intended for the "release, maturing, and fruition of human potentialities," or, as it was put somewhat earlier, "This earth was not built for a chaos, but was designed as an habitation for man."

It would seem to be necessary, therefore, to say what kind of Christianity we are talking about. And it would

91

seem to be necessary also to determine what elements in Christianity are likely to furnish a spiritual basis for democracy.

In trying to isolate the kind of Christianity which may be vitally related to democracy, it would seem—offhand— to be the type which sees in democracy the goal of religion, discarding all supernatural and otherworldly reference for a humanistic ethic. It is a curious fact, however, that the religion out of which democracy has in part stemmed was supernatural and otherworldly. In other words, if democracy is historically related to Christianity, the relation is to a religion—as formerly understood—not to a democratic ethic conceived by modern sophisticates. And this simple historical fact cannot, I believe, be evaded by assuming that there is some one ethical principle—such as sympathy or good will—which has combined with some other abstract ideas to form democracy. Most historians who have lived beyond the nineteenth century feel that historic Christianity cannot be treated like a chemical formula. Christianity was—let us hope it also is—a living religion, not an aggregate of disparate beliefs.

But when this is clear, one should remember that some forms of Christianity have been so devoted to what is called the soul and its relation to another world that any reference to this world seems purely unintentional. Sometimes also the reference to this world has been so completely pietistic that social implications have been lost. In short, if democracy has any relation to historic Christianity, the relation is to those forms of Christianity which are neither entirely humanistic nor entirely otherworldly.

One other observation ought to be made, although it does not fit into current fashions. Historically those forms of Christianity which seem to have prepared people for democracy have been those which laid great stress upon the individual. Today in church and state there is great emphasis upon corporate life and corporate action, and this is as it should be. But a great deal depends upon whether the corpus derives its life from the individuals or the individuals derive their life from the corpus. Here ancient analogies break down, but I do not need to remind a group of theologians and political scientists that a great variety of doctrines can be comprehended under these two categories. Democracy belongs definitely under only one of them.

What is there in Christianity, let us now ask, which may serve as a spiritual basis for democracy? Homiletical attempts to derive the individual's rights to life, liberty, and the pursuit of happiness from the teachings of Jesus are futile. Apparently Jesus did not think much of one's right simply to live; he did not mention liberty; and he seems to have said little about the pursuit of happiness. More modern shibboleths, such as equality, find little more support in his sayings.

A better way to approach our problem is to ask what there is in democracy which seems to depend upon Christianity. And a very good way to get an answer is to look at Christianity through other eyes. In his widely read *Myth of the Twentieth Century*, Rosenberg draws a sharp line between what he holds to be the German and the Christian ethic. According to Rosenberg, the German has as his supreme values honor and duty, while the Christian holds to an ethic of love, meaning humility, subjection, asceticism. The one enables the Germanic peoples to be bound together in a racial state, which Rosenberg holds the only possible one in the modern world; while the other ethic, that of Christianity, prepares people only for the universalism, the humanitarianism, the individualism of a democracy.

93

I have used Rosenberg's book for illustration because it has been very popular in Nazi Germany. But it might just as well have been another book. The Christian doctrine of love has been chosen for attack everywhere an ethic of pride and military ardor has been exalted. Of course one need spend no time in answering the charges that Christian love has always meant submissiveness, or even pacifism. The facts of history take care of such assertions. And every intelligent student of the New Testament or of the church's record knows that Christian love has been truly interpreted, not by the sentimentalists, but by those who hold it against the background of the sterner virtues.

The important fact for our purpose is, however, that the opponents of democracy see the Christian ethic as peculiarly the ethic of democracy. And there is reason for this. Recently there has been much said about the inadequacy of what is called Puritan ethics for an urbanized society, and several gentlemen with more courage than historical information have tried to create an ethic out of equal parts of Benjamin Franklin and Epictetus, spiced with dashes of Plato, *et al.* Actually the Christian ethic itself arose in an urbanized society. It was not the product of the idyllic countryside of Renan's imagination but was a synthesis of the Hebrew morality and the social insights of Jesus supplemented by the experiences of the early church and of its leaders, such as Paul, in the crowded districts of the Mediterranean cities. The Christian ethic is an ethic of cities, of living together with people in an urbanized world. As one of the greatest Christian scholars America ever saw, Professor Arthur Cushman McGiffert, used to say: "The Christian religion is personal, and the Christian ethic is social."

Now, the Fascist offers an alternative to democracy, that of a racial state held together by power and recognizing as supreme values honor and duty. Unquestionably the problem of order in an urbanized society can be solved this way. On the other hand, democracy offers the ideals of universalism, as opposed to racialism; of individualism, in so far as consonant with social welfare; and of humanitarianism. In a democracy these can be achieved only by the free co-operation of the people. Therefore the ethic of democracy is of primary importance. Unless democratic people recognize these ideals and hold to them tenaciously, the democratic way of life is obviously doomed. And this is precisely the line of attack which the Fascist propagandist takes. He makes his first assault upon the Christian ethic, which he recognizes as the strategic center of the democratic state.

But in democracy there is also a place for self-denial, as well as for the universalism and humanitarianism of which we hear so much. Not only is the democratic political society *for* the people, but it is also *by* the people. And this means that there must be self-denial, a regard for the weaker members of society, a willingness to go just as fast as the majority of men, including the weak mentally and morally, can be persuaded to go. This means that good men desirous of perfection must move forward only as the majority of men can be persuaded to go along. In other words, the only utopia possible to democracy is that which the majority desires and achieves for itself. The audacity of proposing that the majority of any group of men be persuaded to such moral heights is enough to appall the most idealistic of men. And yet this is precisely what we propose to do. Certainly it takes great moral courage to be a democrat. And to imagine that religion has no place in such a program is to know little of human nature.

Democracy is rooted in the Christian ethic. But let us go further and ponder the raw fact that democracy is under attack. It is for others to consider the attacks upon democracy based upon its failure to go far enough. Of these there have been plenty. But our concern at the present is with those who assert that democracy *per se* is bad, that it is outmoded and must go, along with eight per cent interest and the hooped skirt. There have always been critics, of course, as those who remember their Carlyle well know; but now the criticism is from both the Left and the Right; and the criticism on one side is implemented by the most formidable armies in history. We do not have time now to discuss whether democracy may not be extended more fully; we are too busy trying to decide whether we shall have any democracy at all. When the winds blow and the floods descend, the question is whether the house will stand, not whether the interior decorator has fumbled his colors.

Today the question whether democracy should be saved has become what the theologians call an "existential" question. It directly affects me and all that I have. It may mean the life or death of my son. Why should I risk everything to save democracy, to provide that there may be the "release, maturing, and fruition of the potentialities of human nature"? Here we are at the nub of the matter. "The case at bottom," says Mr. Laski, "is an ethical one. It postulates that the right to happiness is inherent in man as a member of society and that any system which denies that right cannot be justified." And Mr. Dewey says the same. "We have to see that democracy means the belief that humanistic culture should prevail; we should be frank and open in our recognition that the proposition is a moral one—like any idea that concerns what *should* be." And he means by humanistic culture, culture based on faith in the potentialities of human nature. But on what do we base our belief in human nature, on the right of people

96

to be "happy"—understood, of course, in the broad sense of the word?

Certainly there is very little in the present scene to encourage such faith in human nature that we should risk our all upon it. If our novelists, glorying in their discoveries about human nature—discoveries which they might have found set forth in somewhat better English in the King James Version of Paul's Epistles—have not already done so, the stories of Rotterdam and of Coventry and of the Russian front will surely convince us that man is a brutal and terrible creature.

It is true that some case for democracy may be made out from history. It would seem, on the whole, that democratic countries have done more to release the potentialities of human nature. But to hear our critics, particularly the starry-eyed idealists, we are wallowing in such a slough of iniquity that there is no health left in us. Of course some of our most idealistic leaders seem to have got a democratic society on earth mixed up with the New Jerusalem, and some allowance should be made for that. But at the best, democracy has not had time nor yet the quality of human intelligence and morality to achieve that society which would definitely prove the case.

The truth is that Dewey and Laski are right: at bottom this matter of democracy rests upon a moral choice; it is one of the things that we cling to because it *should* be. But, Mr. Dewey and Mr. Laski notwithstanding, the things to which men cling because they should be are those which men believe to have some ultimate character. In the statement written by the Founding Fathers, which is now coming again into fashion, it was said that "we hold these truths to be self-evident, that all men are created equal; that they are endowed by their Creator with certain unalienable rights; that among these are life, liberty and the pursuit of happiness." It is, of course, easy to quibble about the sincerity of this statement, but it is safer to assume that these men meant what they said. They believed that the rights for which they contended were written into the nature of things. In this instance it happened to be human nature, and we can no longer follow them in their psychology. But the essential point to remember is that these founders were not merely leading embattled farmers to protest against high taxes; they were standing for something that to their minds was an essential part of the scheme of things.

We have come to a time when the whole democratic conception is being thrown out by no small part of the nations of the world. It is true that this has not been a reasonable choice, for no nation with any considerable democratic experience has as yet deliberately rejected democracy. But neither is the attack upon democracy a mere incident in the imperialistic career of the little Caesars. From Karl Marx to the latest confused despiser of the herd, there is an attack upon the idea of democracy which will not perish with the end of this war. It is essential, therefore, that we inquire whether our democratic notions are simply the products of our environment plus some suggestions from a classical education now rapidly disappearing, or whether democracy does correspond to something which we believe rooted in the nature of things.

Here religion has a word. For a very respectable part of the Christian world believes that Christianity teaches a regard for human personality which is not satisfied with the saving of the soul in a future paradise but demands the release of human potentialities here. True, those who believe that the Reformation symbols are the most perfect expression of the Christian faith sometimes talk as if man is totally corrupt and there is no good in him. And it is

98

difficult for any Christian to escape the belief that the true achievement of man is by the spirit of God. But so far as man's political life is concerned there is always the doctrine of the Natural Law which even Paul called in to explain the life of the Gentile in government. Moreover, it is to be remembered that, while men are as nothing in the sight of God, they are not necessarily negligible in relation to each other. In short, mankind is of infinite worth, whether potentially as a child of God, or actually, as some theologians would have it. Either way we take it, the Christian regards the place of man in the scheme of things as a part of the divine ordering. And those Christians who believe man of such worth that government should be "of the people, by the people, for the people," hold this not as self-evident, not on the basis of some theory of history, not as a hypothesis of a pragmatic philosophy, but as a corollary of their faith in God. I state this baldly, because it is fashionable to derive democracy from a blend of Platonic belief in reason, Stoic universalism, and Christian love or sympathy. It cannot be too often repeated that the Christian's belief in the worth of the individual is not a derivative from an ethical principle but is an integral part of his religion.

It would appear, then, that democracy rests upon the Christian ethic, our enemies themselves being witnesses. Whether an ethic unsupported by religion is sufficient to bear the attacks of racial bigotry, arrogance, ambition, greed, and all the rest is another matter. And it is another matter also whether groups which are educated to recognize their rights, but are not yet educated to secure them by democratic processes, can acquire the patience necessary for democracy from ethical teaching alone. To many of us it would appear that only a mighty core of religious people can hold a democracy together.

99

And in the disillusionment which is certain to follow this war, when the idealists who hoped that the kingdom would be restored to Israel preach cynicism to a tired people, it will require a great faith to maintain democracy. Perhaps exhortations to moral preferences may suffice. But it is more likely that the democratic faith will live among those who believe that it has a value which, as Sir Thomas Browne said of the soul, "was before us and will be after us."

Factors in World Order

CHRISTIANITY AND THE RACE PROBLEM

Gonzalo Báez-Camargo
Executive Secretary, National Evangelical Council of Mexico

THE WORLD IN WHICH WE ARE LIVING TODAY IS TORN BY A violent struggle. Several nations are fighting to maintain their free existence against others whose ambition is to become the supreme rulers of mankind. Of this ambition the idea of racial superiority is a fundamental element. It has become a fanatical belief.

On the other hand, we see everywhere the signs of racial unrest. Races heretofore held under subjection are questioning the rights of their rulers. They are becoming conscious of their right to a free, self-determined life. The fact that in some cases white domination has been paternal rather than ruthless possibly makes the situation less acute but none the less serious. The subject races are coming of age; and the idea of a permanent tutorage over them, even by the best of friends, they strongly resent.

Let us not deceive ourselves. Violent and crazy as it may have become in the Third Reich, racism is not a German monopoly. Racial prejudice is a universal evil. Not only do white nations consider themselves generally superior, but also those deemed by the white as inferior establish their own categories among themselves.

Our democracies are deeply infected with the poison of racism. Let us not give our enemies the satisfaction of whispering it into the ears of our racial minorities. Let us be

101

the first to bring this fact out into the open and face it as men. And not only our democracies but our churches are infected as well. That race prejudice and race discrimination exist in our midst while at the same time we fight against German racism and undertake to carry the gospel of brotherhood to all races of the world is both a challenge to our democracies and a rebuke to our Christianity. Recognition of this fact does not invalidate our rightful fight against racism in the external front, but it places on our shoulders the unavoidable duty to fight it with as much determination in the home front as well.

Why a Race Problem?

I submit that from the very start we make a most important distinction between racism and race. Race, as such, is a subject for objective study. Whether there is such a thing as race and, if so, what the implications are of this fact are questions for anthropology and correlated sciences to answer. Racism, on the contrary, is a belief. It is the belief in the existence of innately superior and inferior races, and in the immanent right of the former to bring the latter into permanent subjection. Racism has nothing to do with scientific research. At times it has claimed the support of science, but it is not really interested in what science has to say. Its final allegation is that the white races must be superior because at present they dominate the world. It is nonscientific. It begs the question.

The truth is that on the question of race racism has forged a myth, a superstition. It is not race, but racism that creates the problem. Racism has inoculated the idea of race with gratuitous and self-exalting implications. It has thus created friction, oppression, and strife. If nature ever established race, we have made an awful problem of it.

102

I have referred to racism as a superstition. I am intent on that word. This means that scientific research, to the best of our knowledge, and the gospel truth, to the best of our understanding, are both strongly opposed to racism.

Is Race a Fact?

The term "race" has been very loosely employed. People speak nonchalantly of white, black, yellow, Anglo-Saxon, Latin, African, European, Asiatic, Teutonic, Jewish, or Scandinavian races. Race is often used as synonymous with color of skin, geographical location, nationality, or language.

Anthropologists find enormous difficulty when the attempt is made to classify human beings. They cannot even agree on the best basis for classification. Color of the skin, form and color of the eyes or of the hair, form and measures of the skull, form of the nose and lips, stature, and other bodily traits have been discarded as a sure mark of race. Southern inhabitants of India, Australian aborigines, Ethiopians, and some natives of the Pacific Islands are black, but do not belong to the Negro group. Dark eyes are found in all human groups. Soft and undulated hair is common to natives of Australia, desert Bedouins, Moors, and European Nordics. Round-headed and long-headed people may be found within the same group, and the same is true of differences in stature and even the form of nose and lips. Observed facts thus lead to the conclusion that these physical traits are uncertain and have only a relative value as a basis of human classification.

The difficulty increases considerably when the attempt is made to appoint intellectual, social, and moral traits as a basis of distinction. The bare fact is that each human group, regardless of how the grouping has been determined, includes a great individual variety in psychological make-up, social trends, and moral quality. The American Psychological Association at its annual meeting in December, 1938, stated that no psychological differences for a fundamental distinction between so-called races have been discovered and, furthermore, that there are no *innate* mental differences between the races.

The conventional conception of race runs against the bulk and weight of scientific evidence. "There is no right to consider human races as biological races," says Marcel Prenant, the French biologist. "Nature does not form races," adds Ameghino, the anthropologist; "it only forms collections of individuals with some resemblances between them." The false conception of race has been forged by theoretically pasting together a number of characteristics more or less frequent in a certain human group. Race becomes thus, as the Argentinian scholar, Dr. Emilio Troise puts it, "an anthropological abstraction." Prejudice often has a very large hand in developing it. Only a very small minority in any group answers to this ideal description. If, for instance, only two traits are taken as the combined definition of the European—for example, color of the eyes and of the hair—recent investigations tell us that as many as 75 per cent of any region in Europe would have to be ruled out. Retzius applied a standard of only three traits to the Swedish people—white skin, blue eyes, and blond hair —and found, to the eternal confusion of all racists, that only 11 per cent met the requirements of the ideal "Swedish type."

But All Men Are Not Equal

What has been said does not mean that there are altogether no differences between human groups. Modern anthropology recognizes the existence of such differences, when taken in general and not in a very strict sense. It is for this reason that scientific circles tend to abandon the use of the word "race" and try substitutes. The purpose is to leave no doubt that, when referring to human groups and to their general differences, no such rigorous distinction as the one associated with the word "race" is in mind.

The pointing out of differences has only a descriptive value and does not imply essential distinctions. In this sense, three general types are more commonly accepted: the Caucasian, the Mongolian, and the Negroid. Such an authority as Dr. Franz Boas, however, prefers only two, the Mongolian and the Negroid, and considers the Caucasian as a local specialization of the Mongolian. A combination of physical traits is considered descriptive of these types, but no basic mental differences are established. These types fall into several subtypes which in turn give way to numerous groupings. Dr. Ralph Linton, of Columbia University, has advanced another view. In his opinion, the only real differences exist between hundreds of smaller groups which he calls "castes," whose members follow more or less closely a given type. All other classifications he considers as "artificial entities" created by the investigator for practical purposes. Dr. Linton admits that human castes indeed show some physiological and mental differences.

Human Differences No Basis for Racism

A close study of the nature and meaning of whatever differences may exist between men shows that no racist ideas can be validly founded upon them. In the first place, these differences are secondary. They may be as superficial as the color of skin, hair, or eyes. The size and form of the skeleton are not so different as might be supposed. Modern science does not accept a strict correlation between intelligence and the size and form of the skull.

Differences are not as wide and important between men as between varieties of animals belonging to the same species. There are more real differences between a bulldog and a pekingese than between an Englishman and a Chinese.

Differences are individual rather than racial. A great variety of physical as well as of psychological types is found within any given group, be it national or "racial." Once a certain set of characteristics is fixed as typical, more exceptions are found than cases following the alleged rule.

Most of the differences are acquired rather than innate, when a group is considered as a whole. These differences may be real mutations, due to the influence of the environment. It seems now well established, for instance, that color of the skin depends on the intensity and composition of the sun rays. Actinic rays, more abundant and strong in some parts of the world, particularly near the equator, require a dark pigmentation, while solar radiations in the north make a light color of the skin more adequate for survival. Because of its habitat, after a long period of time, a human group develops and transmits by heredity a certain color of the skin.

The present diversity of physical human types is due, then, as Dr. Linton explains, to variations caused by the environment and the joint action of a natural tendency to vary, natural selection, and favorable conditions for the fixation of the acquired traits.

But the most important fact about differences is that they do not imply a question of inferiority-superiority in a permanent sense. Biological, intellectual, and emotional differences, when they exist, are not strict and immutable.

The environment, especially education, may change them. On the other hand, a certain human group may combine traits indicative both of an "inferior" or a "superior" development. This is true even in the physical sense. For instance, apes have flat noses, thin lips, and straight hair. It would seem, then, that the Negro is less advanced in evolution than the white if we consider his nose, but not so if his lips and hair are regarded.

Summing up the findings of science on this matter, Dr. Arnold Toynbee says that the alleged racial explanation of human differences is either foolishness or imposture.

Culture Is Not Inherited

When we speak of a "cultural heritage," we must warn ourselves not to understand that the cultural achievements of our ancestors have been passed down to us "by blood," that is, by the laws of heredity. The American Anthropological Association, meeting in December, 1938, declared that there is no scientific basis for distinctions meaning racial inferiority and that although "some similar physical variations" in large groups are inherited, the inheritance of psychological and cultural traits is not confirmed by science.

The culture of a human group, as the culture of an individual, is transferable only by education. There is no mysterious immanent transmission by blood of the cultural achievements of the group. The "son of a noble race" must yet learn to be personally noble.

Culture Is Not the Achievement of a Unique Race

"In scientific language, culture is not the function of the race," says Miss Ruth Benedict. Not all the groups of a given race have achieved a uniform type of culture, and in the building of civilizations groups belonging to several races have participated.

Races deemed inferior or found backward at a given time have had or may have their own day. The culture we enjoy today is the result of peoples of different racial stock. We owe much to the Greeks, but the Greeks learned from the Egyptians and Chaldeans; steel was first produced in India or Turkestan; the Chinese invented gunpowder, paper, and printing; together with India, China has also given us lofty ethics and philosophy, literature and art; several Semitic groups gave great impulse to industry, commerce, philosophy, and poetry. The Arabs were the wise men of the Middle Ages. They developed algebra, made amazing scientific discoveries, produced great philosophers and poets. Even the American Indians, lacking the contact with other civilizations, were able to create cultures as advanced as the Toltec, the Maya, and the Inca.

The capacity for the creation of highly developed cultures is not a monopoly of one "superior" race, and there are no races crippled and made impotent by nature to achieve a high degree of culture.

Race Supremacy Is Incidental, Not Natural

Indeed, in every age we see races and nations at different levels of culture. Some are backward, others are flourishing. Some are rapidly advancing, while still others decay. But there is no question of natural race superiority involved in this picture. The cultural supremacy that a certain race achieves at a given time is determined by a combination of historic, geographic, social, religious, and educational factors. Its success is no evidence that the other races are born inferior or destined, by a special decree of Providence, to remain perpetually backward.

The very idea of race superiority is vague and relative. Physical tests show, for instance, that in Africa the Negro is stronger than the white, because he resists the hardships of life in the jungle better. In a recent study, quoted by Miss Benedict, Otto Klineberg found that indeed Negroes show a lower I.Q. when compared with whites living in the same neighborhood, but that Negroes living in a more progressive environment in turn show a higher I.Q. than white residents of backward communities. Physical and mental tests, then, must take into account differences in physical environment, education, social conditions, and such.

Race superiority, says Dr. Linton, is a social myth, not a biological fact. Old Cicero used to say, "Men differ by what they learn, but they are equal in their ability to learn; there is no race that, guided by reason, cannot attain virtue."

Mixture of Races—Improvement or Degeneration?

The common idea is that races, in order to keep strong, must maintain their blood purity and that all mixture of races leads to degeneration. This is the fundamental tenet of German racism, but it is also entertained by other people. No better example can be offered of how plain prejudice may attempt to mask itself under a scientific pretense.

In the first place, only certain scanty, isolated, and undeveloped groups, deep in the mountains of Tibet, the jungles of Africa, the highlands of Amazonia, or icy Cape York, could claim a relative purity of race. It is significant, however, that precisely these groups live in a very primitive and inferior condition. But, as Prenant says, "The term 'pure race,' used in an absolute way, means nothing. . . . . At present, no homogeneous peoples of

109

GONZALO BAEZ-CAMARGO

pure race exist, if there ever existed any." This statement is fully supported by history. All attempts to maintain "blood purity" have failed. Migrations, wars, vicinity, and commercial intercourse have made human groups mix freely.

On the other hand, all the civilized groups that history knows are, without exception, a mixture of races. Europe has been the greatest mixing caldron. Mongolian and Negroid streams merged with the ancient and already mixed population. But European culture is the mother of modern progress. In this continent, the United States, Argentina, and Brazil are the outstanding witnesses to the strength and cultural creativeness of a racial melting pot.

The myth of half-breed inferiority thus falls by its own weight. The present inferior condition of some mixed groups is not due to a fatal curse in the crossing of bloods nor to a biological degeneration, which cannot be scientifically proved, but to race prejudice, inferior education, and other social handicaps. When somebody points to that inferior condition as a proof that the mixture of races results in degeneration, he is bluntly begging the question.

It seems, on the contrary, that half-breeds are generally more prolific, so much so that in order to raise the index of natality of a country that needs it, some authorities in demographic problems recommend intermarriage. Some mixed types, the Eurasian, for instance, show remarkable beauty and vitality. On the whole, half-breeds are neither superior nor inferior to the so-called pure races. Given the same opportunities and placed under the same conditions, they show as much ability and creativeness.

Not being able to find scientific bases for their contention that "race must be kept clean of blood infection"—a favorite expression of Hitler's—many insist on a dis-

110

crimination of races "desirable" and "undesirable" for intermarriage. All kinds of arguments claimed to be drawn from eugenics, laws of Mendel, cross-fertilization, and such are used. But this is only another and more "honorable" disguise of prejudice. A declaration made by the Third International Congress on Genetics (Edinburgh, 1939) is to the effect that genetic transformations depend on changes in social circumstances and human attitudes.

There are undesirable individuals for intermarriage, on account of physical or mental disease, but these individuals are found in all races. To speak of undesirable and desirable races is an undue generalization. Immigration and marriage laws, as well as social rules, should discriminate, when they must, not upon a racial but entirely upon an individual basis. And as for the extension of the Mendelian laws of breeding to human beings, suffice it to bring forward the authorized statement of Prenant, who says that "genetics must not be applied to men except with extreme caution." This is true, because men are men, not mice.

"Of One Blood All Nations of Men"

I have dealt at some length with the race problem in the light of scientific research, even at the risk of giving the impression that I am keeping away from the subject of this lecture as it is stated. My intention has been to dispose first of any possible sniping from behind a "scientific" camouflage.

The Federal Council of Churches well expresses the fundamental position of Christianity with regard to the race problem. It says, "Christian teaching about the essential unity of the human race as created by God and as redeemed by Christ is so clear that there really can be no controversy about its meaning."

111

Christianity teaches that the human race is essentially one because it has a common origin and one is the Creator of all. The book of Genesis tells of an original couple. Whether this story is taken literally or not, its meaning seems clear: the Bible teaches the common origin of mankind. Modern anthropology speaks likewise of a single primitive human type. In other words, all human beings belong to the same species.

In spite of its story of a chosen people, the Old Testament holds to the same doctrine. Job refers to class struggle, but to race conflict as well, when he exclaims: "If I did despise the cause of my manservant or of my maidservant, when they contended with me; what then shall I do when God riseth up? and when he visiteth, what shall I answer him? Did not he that made me in the womb make him? and did not one fashion us in the womb?" This is also stressed by the prophet Malachi: "Have we not all one father? hath not one God created us?"

In his address upon the Areopagus, Paul voiced the same teaching: "And [God] hath made of one blood all nations of men." The most absurd theory that our times have seen arise is that of the superiority of a certain blood in a racial sense. No matter what Hitler says or the Red Cross believes when making discriminations for its blood bank, that theory finds absolutely no support on scientific research and is diametrically opposed to Christian doctrine. It is pure superstition.

Superior blood quality can be established only by analysis of its composition and has nothing to do with race as such. Malnutrition and disease, of course, result in a reduction of red corpuscles and alteration of the proportion of other blood components. It is only in this strict bio-

112

logical sense that we are permitted to speak of superior and inferior blood, but there is an individual and pathological, not a racial, line between the two.

"Of one blood all nations of men." This is the unmistakable teaching of Christianity. Being a Jew himself, Jesus, as Dr. Rollin H. Walker has said, "did not for a moment believe that there was something in Jewish blood that constituted them essentially superior to other nations." Nor in any other blood, Jew, Greek or "Aryan," Nordic or Latin, white or black, American or Asiatic.

"One God and Father of All"

But for Christianity the main foundation for the unity of mankind is the universal fatherhood of God. John the Baptist had taught that even stones could become children of Abraham if God so wished. This is also a central teaching of Christ and of the Apostles. When the Jewish leaders stressed, as a basis for racial discrimination, that they were children of Abraham, Jesus fearlessly pointed up to a higher fatherhood which embraced all men.

All men are essentially equal, because all are born of one Father, who made them all in his own image and likeness. This common seal of divine identity makes of mankind a single family. Deeper than the skin-deep differences in color or the configuration of hair and skull, even deeper than all present differences in background, physical strength, cultural development, and moral excellency, this inner resemblance is to be found in all men; and it is this resemblance that makes all men equal. The universal fatherhood of God means the universal brotherhood of men. "*Our* Father which art in heaven." And to all races that pride calls "inferior" and therefore destined to bondage Christianity sends a forthright message of libera-

113

tion—social and national as well as spiritual—in the words of Paul, "Wherefore thou art no more a servant, but a son."

"Who Gave Himself a Ransom for All"

But, according to Christianity, mankind is one not only because of a common human ancestry, a common divine Creator, a common inner image, and a common Father, but also because of a common Redeemer. All men, regardless of race or class, are sinners. All men are impotent to justify themselves in the sight of God. All men stand in need of supernatural redemption. For all men Christ died. This is the gospel. And it is this common Fountain of Health, where all men have to drink in order to live, that establishes strong bonds of solidarity between all.

The fact that in the supreme hour of instituting the Redemption God makes no discriminations, racial or otherwise, but offers salvation to all men strictly on the same basis constitutes the final and strongest condemnation of all our prejudices, and gives us the very substance and key of human unity as well as the most powerful motive for race reconciliation. "I perceive that God is no respector of persons"; this was Peter's great discovery in the field of race relations. And it is in allusion to this common Redeemer that Paul addresses another race, the Gentiles. Let us hear, in the modern rendering of Dr. Weymouth, these wonderful words, the highest Christian code and doctrine on the race problem:

Therefore, do not forget that formerly you were Gentiles as to your bodily condition. . . . . But now in Christ Jesus you who once were so far away have been brought near through the blood of Christ.

114

For He is our peace—He who has made Jew and Gentile one, and in His own human nature has broken down the hostile dividing wall. . . . . His design was to unite the two sections of humanity in Himself so as to form one new man, thus effecting peace, and to reconcile Jew and Gentile in one body to God, by means of His cross—slaying by it their mutual enmity. So He came and proclaimed the Gospel of peace to you who were so far away, and peace to those who were near; because it is through Him that Jew and Gentile alike have access through one Spirit to the Father.

You are therefore no longer mere foreigners or persons excluded from civil rights. On the contrary, you share citizenship with the saints and are members of His family.

Christ is our peace, peace and love between the races. It is difficult to understand why we Christians have been so stubborn in resisting the full implications of this message we claim to accept; why, while we sing, "In the cross of Christ I glory," we still hesitate to carry into practice the truth that the other races and our race are made "in one body to God, by means of His cross"; why we still suffer the existence, not only in our communities but within our own churches, of "dividing walls" and lines between the races.

The Supreme Worth of the Human Person, Regardless

Nothing is more obvious in the life and teachings of Christ than that he was fundamentally opposed to race discrimination. He came to a nation full of race pride and prejudice. It was racism in its most typical manifestations—civil, economic as well as religious—that he was called to meet. And he met it consistently and courageously. Once and again he was not afraid to run counter to racial prejudice. Illustrations of this fact in the gospel story are too well known to need quotation in full. His

115

gentle approach to the Samaritan woman, his brave commendation of the faith of the Gentiles, his own preaching outside the boundaries of Israel, and the superb and revolutionary parable of the good Samaritan may be mentioned as typical of his attitude and message.

Jesus insisted on regarding man as man, apart from any racial, social, and even moral discriminations. For him every man was a child of God, taken away from his Father by the power and bondage of sin, and needing the supreme touch of redemptive love. During his ministry to all men, he consciously broke all existing regulations based on racial and social discrimination, whether imposed by specific laws or merely by social conventions. He mixed with all men freely. He considered all men essentially equal. Peter, who had accompanied Jesus for three years, was very slow indeed in understanding his teaching. He needed a special vision before he could say, "But God hath shewed me that I should not call any man common or unclean"; and then he was still afraid of practicing this vision fully, and Paul had to rebuke him in public.

The central teaching of Jesus is that every man, every human person, is of infinite worth in the sight of God, regardless of race, culture, or social standing. As Dr. T. R. Glover once said, according to a quotation by Bishop Kern, "You may have race prejudice if you want it; or you may have Jesus if you want him; but you cannot have both."

Christianity and Human Groupings

All that has gone before does not mean that Christianity ignores the historic fact that there exist many human groupings in the form of nations, each one a family of men bound together by common tradition, purpose, and tasks; but it never gives much significance to the division of men in races. In Christ "there is neither Greek nor Jew, ... Barbarian, Scythian." Neither does Christianity ignore such differences as may exist between individuals or groups. Paul's complete saying was: "And [God] hath made of one blood all nations of men for to dwell on all the face of the earth, having determined their appointed seasons [as one rendering reads], and the bounds of their habitation."

Here we see the hand of God in history and the existence of nations as ordained by him. It seems that, as is the case with the family, the larger family of the nation is also a part of the plan of God for the development of mankind on earth. He also, according to Paul, appoints their "seasons." The season of a nation is the time when it flourishes and achieves power and influence. This seems, at first sight, a dangerous concession to the nationalism of "manifest destiny" and world domination. But it is not so. It is simply another way of stating the Christian doctrine of vocations.

Christianity recognizes vocations in nations as well as in individuals. According to his designs, God chooses individuals, and also nations, for special missions, and endows them with the gifts that are necessary to carry them out. Such was the teaching of the Old Testament prophets, and the New Testament does not invalidate it. In this fact lies the tragic mystery of Israel, the Chosen People. In this sense—as illustrated by the parable of the talents—Christianity admits the existence of differences between the various human groups as between individuals.

But this Christian doctrine of different vocations and gifts does not imply essential superiority or the right to dominate. Vocations and gifts simply mean a greater responsibility to serve. What Jesus said of individuals holds as good in the case of nations. They must serve, not be served. Sense of divine commission should lead to humility, not pride. For when God chooses a nation for a special task and bestows upon it special gifts and opportunities, he does so in order that it may become not a ruler but a servant of mankind, and that through its achievements the rest of mankind may also be enriched. Differences in nations, then, must be considered as differences in vocations; in the plan of God all vocations are equally important, and he only is greater who renders more and greater services to others. It is only then that, as Bishop Kern has said, "Differences do not necessarily divide; they may enrich." They *do* enrich.

This reference, of course, is to nations and not to races. But I have gone into it because so many people think of their race in national terms. The fact is, however, that a Christian may be—and rightly so, if it is in the spirit of the gospel—fully devoted to his nation, whereas for a Christian to be race-conscious, to behave in terms of race distinctions and race devotion, is not only unscientific but entirely inconsistent with his Christian profession. It is nothing but a compromise with superstition, with heathen worship of the blood, and with un-Christian social prejudices.

German Racism Defeated—Then What?

The defeat of German racism is clearly not enough. Let us face the problem that will still be awaiting us. Men of all races are fighting under the leadership of white races against racism. These men are being told that German racism is crazy, that there are no inferior races, that freedom and self-determination must be enjoyed by all. These men are listening to these exhortations and are gallantly fighting for them. Then, when German racism is defeated and these men go home, shall they find that their people are subjected, by those to whose banner of freedom and equality they rallied, to abuses of the same kind, even if not in the same degree, as those practiced by the people against which they were led to fight? Shall we then ask these men to quench, all at once, this beautiful fire of liberty which we have kindled in their hearts in order to make good fighters of them?

What Shall We Do, Then?

We must ask ourselves honestly whether after all "white supremacy" is an end in itself or whether the other races should be helped to attain their full development in a climate of good will, friendship, and mutual service. A racial adjustment after the war is impending. It is simply a question of which we shall let rule it, the worldly principle of violent strife or the Christian principle of co-operation and love.

The things that should be done are obvious. The problem is not that we do not know what to do. It is rather that we lack the courage for doing it. For it means breaking with prejudices of long standing, meeting fierce opposition, exposing ourselves to abuse and suffering, in other words, taking up our cross. But Christians cannot help solve the race problem except by the way of the cross.

In the first place, it is imperative for the white people to take the initiative. A thorough change of attitude toward other races must be brought about. In order to achieve it, it is necessary to undertake an intense educational drive. Public conscience and opinion must be led to understand that race discriminations are ultimately unjust. To this end all educational means at our disposal must be used: the school, the press, the radio, public

119

speech, moving pictures, and practical projects in inter-racial friendship.

At the same time we must fight for the elimination of all legal, social, educational, and economic discriminations based on race. Discriminating laws must be abolished. The same educational facilities must be offered to all; and in the case of racial groups which, for economic or other reasons, find difficulty in taking advantage of these facilities, special provisions must be made in order to encourage and assist them. A well-organized crusade must be launched for the demolition of social race barriers and of all customs or regulations that place some groups at economic disadvantage on account of their race. All vocations must be entirely open to racial minorities: the liberal professions, industrial management, service in the civil and armed forces of the nation, and other legal occupations, as well as the ordinary trades.

The whole system of wardship must be revised. Although provisions must be made for the protection of racial minorities against exploitation by more advanced groups, these provisions should be based upon the principle that wardship can be only a provisional expedient. No racial minority should be deemed as permanently inferior and therefore as permanent wards. This treatment, even granting that it be truly benevolent, may result in the stifling of creativeness, self-respect, and the attaining of self-government, so necessary for the full development of human personality. Only when racial minorities are accepted as full members of the community and freely merge into it can they bring out their maximum contribution to the welfare of all and achieve the fullness of social life. By keeping them apart the feeling of their isolation is dangerously deepened. In assuming their wardship the state takes upon itself also the duty to promote

120

the education and development of the racial minorities so that they may attain as soon as possible to full age and cease to be wards in order to become real citizens. Appreciation of the native capacities, art, folklore, and ways of life peculiar to these minorities must not result in their isolation and a perpetuation of their lower condition.

The Church Must Lead

There is no body in the world today for which the duty to lead the way towards the solving of the race problem becomes more imperative than for the church. The church is in possession of a faith and a teaching in which the essential unity of the human race and the longing to see it develop into a real brotherhood of love is a central element—in fact, its very substance. The root and motive of this faith are laid much deeper than is the case with any non-Christian and purely humanitarian ethics. This faith is rooted in and motivated by the love of God.

The church *must lead* not only because it is its duty. The church *must lead* because the race problem becomes an acid test of the depth and sincerity of its claims. Racial minorities at home and in the mission fields have every right to make of this issue the supreme test for the church.

The church *must lead*, first, by its own attitude and practice. As the Madras Conference said, "The church must purge its own life of any racial discrimination. . . . . We urge that Christians free themselves from race hatred and easy acquiescence in popular prejudices which lend unconscious support to such [race] persecutions." This was also stressed by the Federal Council of Churches, in one of the statements at its last biennial meeting:

The church must find ways of emphasizing the unity of mankind in its own fellowship. Segregation in the church

121

is a glaring contradiction of the claims of the church to be a fellowship. The church by becoming in fact a fellowship across racial lines—and there has been definite improvement here within the past two decades—can help to solve the general problem of race relations.

Effort to apply this conviction calls for a revision of the present church organization with regard to racial groups. Separate church organizations, sometimes advocated on the claim that they provide race minorities with an opportunity for self-expression, may result rather in a deeper sense of separation, and may become in fact a convenient disguise of actual discrimination. Except when a real problem of language is involved, as in the case of immigrants who have not been assimilated—and language is not strictly coextensive or synonymous with race—the local Christian church, as well as the larger denominational body, should be in itself a real fellowship including members of all the races represented in the community. Such a fellowship would be mutually enriching. This feeling prevailed in some of the discussions of the Madras Conference.

Considerable progress has been achieved in the mission fields by helping to develop native leaders and to build up indigenous churches. This process must be encouraged by all possible means. The ideal of an indigenous church, however, must not be understood as necessarily implying that all co-operation with the older churches should cease. Such a course would only substitute the evil of racial isolation for the evil of racial preponderance, and the result would be as harmful for the life of the church as a world fellowship.

The church *must lead* also by its courageous support of all measures and movements directed at the elimination

122

of race discrimination. As Madras said, "The church should exert its influence on the side of all movements working for the full and equal sharing by all races in the common life of mankind." This calls not only for brave pronouncements, but still more for systematic action on the part of the church.

The church *must lead* by its educational program. Deep and permanent change in attitude and spirit can be wrought only by Christian education. The curriculum should include not only more systematic instruction on race and the Christian doctrine of universal brotherhood, but especially more frequent planned experiences of interracial fellowship. I am not stressing here certain "works of benevolence" in which members of a more privileged racial group limit themselves to occasional or regular gifts to underprivileged racial minorities. The danger in such a type of work is that the superior-inferior relation may remain, and pity instead of real love may become the motivation. Much tact must be exercised in order not to give the impression that the other races are still treated as inferior as charities are bestowed on them. True fellowship must be natural, on equal terms, involving a give-and-take relation, mixing in social life, mutual service, and appreciation of the good things the others have. "Do me a favor!" is often the best way of treating people who have been mistreated as inferior, rather than, "Look here, poor fellow, I am going to do you a favor!" This was the secret in the wise approach of Jesus to the Samaritan woman. It is good Christianity as well as sound psychology.

It Must Be Done NOW

The church must undertake this leadership at once, cost what it may. We just cannot afford to wait until after the war. We must decide once for all whether we

123

are to reconcile ourselves with a continuation of racial prejudice and conflict in the postwar world, or whether we resolve to deal with these evils squarely and bravely and endeavor to prevent them from carrying their misery and injustice into the freer, better world order we seek to build.

It is a fine sign of the new awareness of the church to the race problem that individuals and groups are giving themselves to earnest study preliminary to vigorous action. But still more has to be done in order to enlist and mobilize the whole church in this direction.

ECONOMIC FREEDOM

JOHN B. CONDLIFFE

Professor of Economics, University of California, Berkeley

FREEDOM FROM FEAR AND FREEDOM FROM WANT ARE THE political and economic principles to which the United Nations are committed. The statement of such principles is important in itself. Men need ideals to guide their decisions, and symbols, even slogans, in which those ideals may be dramatized. The essential driving force of any action is will, and the common will cannot be mobilized by appeal to reason only, still less to the necessarily complex and routine detail of political and economic action. The old song is true—"It's love, it's love that makes the world go round." Without emotional drive, disciplined and directed by reason, little can be accomplished in our personal or civic lives. It is of the utmost importance, therefore, that our common ideals be pitched high and pitched true. The wagon may bump along an earthy road, but it must be hitched to a star.

It is perhaps worth noting the original meaning of these words "economic freedom." The adjective "economic" is derived from two Greek words meaning "household" and "management." "Political economy," therefore, is the art of national housekeeping. "Freedom" has its root in the same idea. The Saxon word was applied to one who was a member of the household as distinct from a slave. The original and true meaning of "freedom," therefore, is the state of being dear, or valued, or cherished, being a member of a family. Freedom does not mean anarchy. It means a valued share in, and contribution to, organized social life. To state freedom from want as the economic objective of United Nations policy is a simple return to first principles, an assertion of the essential dignity of the individual human being and his right to share in the privileges and responsibilities of a decent social order.

It is one thing, however, to state such an ideal and quite another to work out in practical detail the means of approaching it. It is, moreover, much easier to get agreement in principle on an ideal stated in vague, general terms than it is to get agreement on the action necessary to realize the ideal. The ideal of freedom is not easy to realize in any social group—a family, a nation, or the family of nations. Patience, understanding, tolerance, adjustment, and even sacrifice of individual comfort and convenience are called for. Without these adjustments and sacrifices the greatest happiness of the greatest number cannot be achieved, but it is always difficult for those who must make the adjustments and sacrifices to accept their necessity.

The realization of economic freedom must always be the result of a judicious balance between orderly regulation on the one hand and individual initiative and choice within that regulation on the other. Even in the heyday of what Adam Smith called "the system of natural liberty" there was always an overriding system of law regulating economic activity—the law of property, of contract, of incorporation, of limited liability, supplemented later by legislation regarding working hours, working conditions, and wages. Such legislation, however, must be constantly revised if it is to cope with changing technology and to prevent the growth of new forms of privilege.   Freedom cannot be ensured by clinging to the *status quo*.

Governments have increasingly recognized also that preventive measures to protect individuals from misfortune beyond their individual control are politically right and economically wise.   The most democratic countries in both the Old and the New World—such countries as Denmark and New Zealand—have pioneered this extension of social policy.   No one who knows these countries can believe that their systems of widespread popular education, care for the aged, assistance to widows and orphans, to the sick and the injured, have weakened their moral fiber or impaired their sturdy individualism.   They have high living standards and are among the countries with the highest production and the greatest share in world trade.   What is sometimes called social security is bound to be adopted in increasing measure by all democratic countries.   The Beveridge report is evidence of this.   After all, it is simple common sense, the best of all investments, to ensure the physical and mental health and vigor of a country's most important capital— its working population.   Long ago, in a debate on the Ten Hours Bill in 1847, Macaulay stated a fundamental truth when he said:

Never will I believe that what makes a population stronger, and healthier, and wiser, and better can ultimately make it poorer.   You try to frighten us by telling us that, in some German factories, the young work seventeen hours in the twenty-four, that they work so hard that among thousands there is not one who grows to such a stature that he can be admitted into the army; and you ask whether, if we pass this bill, we can possibly hold our own against such competition as this?   Sir, I laugh at the thought of such competition.   If ever we are forced to yield the foremost place among commercial nations, we shall yield it, not to a race of degenerate dwarfs, but to some people pre-eminently vigorous in body and in mind.

The most important extension of social welfare legislation in recent years has been in the field of employment. The scale of industry has grown, and the complexity of specialized production has increased, while the frontier of settlement has disappeared. Industry has been swept also by periodic crises which in recent years have thrown millions of workers into idleness through no fault of their own. Positive measures—the placement and retraining of skills, the improvement by all available means of labor mobility —are now essential to minimize the deterioration and disheartenment which are the worst features of widespread and prolonged unemployment. But insurance is also necessary to tide the worker over what might otherwise be disaster for him, for his family, and for the community—disaster, let us be clear, that is beyond his individual control.

In addition to social welfare legislation, modern governments have embarked upon public ownership and operation, by various methods, of certain essential services. The first hesitating steps in this direction have now become firmly lodged in the good will and acceptance of democratic communities. We sometimes forget that public education was fiercely assailed by many eminent and distinguished statesmen and scholars. The outstanding opponent of the first education bill introduced into the British Parliament was the Archbishop of Canterbury. It is interesting to speculate what he would think of the great statesman who now sits in his chair at Lambeth. The first efforts to provide adequate supplies of pure water to the growing industrial towns met similar opposition. And so did the first drainage and sanitation systems and the beginnings of public health inspection. There will always in our time be a debatable area—an indeterminate zone—where the merits and demerits of public, as distinct from private, enterprise are hotly discussed. This is how democracy works. But the zone of public enterprise has tended to expand and seems likely to expand further. London has its Transport Authority and New York its Port Authority. The Tennessee Valley Authority has demonstrated that public enterprises can be decentralized and taken out of politics. It has also demonstrated that such enterprises can be used to supplement and promote rather than stifle individual initiative. What can and ought to be done more efficiently by public rather than private enterprise will naturally depend upon civic conditions in different countries at different times. New Zealand did not hesitate from the start to nationalize its water power and develop its hydroelectric energy by government action, but what was possible and wise in that small country with its long tradition of public enterprise may not be so elsewhere.

The fields in which, above all others, controversy has arisen concerning positive action by governments are the related fields of money and credit and public finance. It is inevitable that governments shall control the issue of money. They have always tried to do so. Coinage was a royal prerogative in the Middle Ages. Note issues came under government regulation as soon as it became evident that they were displacing metallic money as common media of exchange. But modern economic activity proceeds in an atmosphere of credit, and in every country effective steps have now been taken to vest the ultimate control of credit policy in official agencies.

The issue of controversy, however, arises concerning the proper use to be made of this power of ultimate control over credit and of the related powers of taxation and public expenditure. Clearly the power to spend from an apparently unlimited purse and if need be to supplement the proceeds of taxation by the creation of new credit places in the hands of governments a potent instrument of social policy. Governments have never hesitated to use this instrument to secure the resources necessary for the prosecution of war. Progressive taxation as an effective means of redistributing real income, though for long resisted as a form of confiscation, is now established practice. In more recent years, however, many governments have used their power, both of taxation and of credit creation, to pursue policies of income redistribution or for other political and social ends—to establish new industries or to prepare for war.

In some democratic countries, particularly in Sweden and Denmark and Australia and New Zealand, successful experiments have been made in flexible policies of credit expansion, correlated with government expenditure, designed to tide the community over the worst effects of severe economic strain generated by financial crises communicated from abroad. Such policies, consciously adopted after democratic debate and carried through as temporary expedients in a crisis, are in fact merely a logical extension of orthodox central banking practice. Their possibilities, and above all their limits, should be carefully studied. They may on occasion be a useful tool, but they are certainly not a panacea. There is no money magic, no easy formula by which a country can escape the necessity of adjusting its economic organization to permanent changes in its international situation merely by printing more pieces of paper or entering larger figures in a bankbook. There have been successful instances of temporary credit expansion in a period of passing difficulty. But history is strewn with cases of disaster where credit expansion has not only failed to avert the necessity of adaptation to changing circumstances, but has ended in inflationary dislocation of economic relationships.

I have deliberately begun this discussion of economic freedom by attempting briefly to analyze the trends of development within national economies. I have defined economic freedom as the achievement of a social order in which the individual citizens have a responsible share, and a valued place, in the economic activity of the national community. To ensure such freedom it is necessary to be vigilant to see that privilege does not grow because technical progress has rendered the legal setting obsolete in some respects. It is necessary also to give every citizen equal opportunity of health, of education, and of employment. And it is necessary, as our society becomes more complex and crowded, for certain common economic activities to be conducted by public enterprise on a social service rather than a profit basis.

I have begun from the national angle because the international problem has no reality apart from national problems. It consists indeed of the interaction of national policies. The most important contribution Americans can make to world stability and prosperity after the war is a stable and prosperous United States, able to help other countries regain their prosperity.

But in this world of ours where airplanes span the oceans and news crackles round the stratosphere, where war has become a peril to the most isolated communities, and where the materials of modern industry must be drawn from the ends of the earth—in such a world national action is not enough. This fact, however far-reaching its implications, ought not to frighten the church that grew from the ministry of the man who wrote in his journal as long ago as June 11, 1739: "I look upon all the world as my parish." Nor should the fact that the reconstruction of international economic relations after this war must take account of the social and political as well as the economic aspirations of nations that have hitherto lagged behind in scientific efficiency and economic organization.

John Wesley, after his soul-searching in Georgia and Germany, pondered the claims of the university as contrasted with those of a comfortable parish, but rejected them both in order to conduct his itinerant ministry in the highways and byways of eighteenth-century England. The societies of Methodism that sprang up struck deepest root in the Midland and Northern counties, where the new factory system was soon to develop. The great new factory towns did not have endowed churches, schools, and universities. Methodism left a permanent mark on their development—on their choral singing, on the fierceness of their democracy, and on the co-operative and trade union movements that developed among them. In no small measure this church has influenced the development of the whole democratic and liberal movement in the country of its origin. It has a great and noble, in some respects a revolutionary, tradition—and certainly a tradition of internationalism—to carry forward.

If we turn, then, to consider the elements of economic freedom as they apply to the international rather than the national economic scene, we are met at once by the striking fact that there exists no world government comparable with the national governments that are able to provide the machinery of law and order, of social security, and of public enterprise. The definition of freedom must be the same. In the family of nations, as in any human family, each people must have a valued and responsible place. But the organized machinery does not exist for the execution of common policies. The loyalties and the will necessary to create that machinery are developing, but for the immediate future we must work through national governments for the achievement of economic freedom. In order that those governments shall not work at cross purposes two conditions are necessary. The first is that the strongest among them shall act responsibly and mercifully toward their weaker neighbors. The second condition is that organs of consultation for the clearing and co-ordination of national policies, and even in certain specific and concrete cases international organs for common action, shall be created.

The best definition of a good-neighbor policy is contained in the answer to the question: "Which now of these three, thinkest thou, was neighbour unto him that fell among the thieves?" The answer was not concerned with the organization of a policing system or with punitive or preventive measures, but, "He that shewed mercy." The tariff and monetary policies followed for domestic reasons by the United States have more important repercussions on other peoples than attendance at international conferences.

The time has gone by when a world trading system operated by free competitive enterprise and guided mainly by the decisions of financial investment on a world-wide scale can be relied upon to maintain a workable economic equilibrium among the nations. The great era of capitalist enterprise in the nineteenth century was a remarkable phase of economic progress. It linked the whole world in a co-operative trading relationship. The economic conquest of this great continent was part of its development. It built great cities in the Far East—Bombay, Calcutta, Singapore, Hong Kong and Shanghai. It "brought a new world into existence to redress the balance of the old"—the new world of the Americas and the British Dominions. It wove all these diverse economies into what has been aptly called "a network of world trade." That network was centered on London. Its trade routes led to and from Europe. Payments were cleared and prices determined in the great financial and commodity markets of Europe, and above all in the London money market.

The stronger new countries profited greatly from this system and did not allow it to deflect them from developing their resources for their own national purposes. They traded on equal terms and made mutually beneficial bargains with their creditors. But many of the industrially backward peoples, and particularly the great Asiatic nations such as India and China, were not able to strike such bargains. They gained on balance, it is true; but their own economic, social, political, and educational progress lagged behind that not only of the West but also of Japan. They now are insistent that the needs of their own people come first, that production be developed for national needs even at some temporary economic cost, that technical training and employment be considered along with profit, that priority be given to industries essential for defense and welfare.

They look to the Western world for help—for needed capital and technical experience. They would prefer to accept such help from the democracies, especially from the United States, which they trust. But there are alternatives. Germany has much to offer them in the way of technical help. Soviet Russia has modernized itself and is now ready to offer its experience. If need be, the Chinese and Indian governments will squeeze the capital necessary to industrialize themselves out of their own hard-driven peoples.

This situation throws down a challenge to our ingenuity

134

and good will. We can, if we are equal to the task, set these great peoples along the road of economic and political development that accords with our own ideal of economic freedom. This is what I understand to be the meaning of the Atlantic Charter. Our administration, together with all the governments of the United Nations, has pledged itself to a co-operative system of expanding world trade and improved living standards. This does not conflict with a national policy of full employment and high living standards. We are not asked to subsidize the world, or to dole out charity to other peoples, as if they were poor relations. Indeed it is essential that our own economy be kept fully employed if we are to be able to help other nations attain the same goal.

What we are asked to do, however, is not to allow special privilege and inefficiency to stand in the way of the common good. If other peoples are to earn the means of buying from us the capital goods necessary for their reconstruction, we must be ready to buy from them. This means that we ought not to allow noncompetitive group interests to shelter behind national protection.

It means, moreover, that we must be ready in the first difficult years of transition from war to peace to discipline and, if need be, ration ourselves so that the scarce supplies of needed materials and foods may be allocated economically. Only in this way can we bring about a balanced restoration of economic activity. We are disciplining ourselves now for war, and in our rationing priorities we, and our Allies too, consider the needs of others as well as our own needs. We do not devote steel to the production of private automobiles because it is needed for tanks and ships to be used on many fronts. We have begun to feel the first mild pinch of food scarcities and even to go colder than we like, so that our armies and the armies of our Allies may be fed and their war machines may not go short of fuel. Is it too much to ask that, for a brief period, a milder version of such rationing be continued in order to achieve orderly and balanced reconstruction of economic activity? In this, as in all instances, we do well to remember that "the quality of mercy is not strained." It is indeed "twice blest," since we cannot maintain our prosperity in any other way.

No one should underestimate the economic ravages of war. Material destruction is the least of them. The enormous productive capacity of modern industry can quickly rebuild shattered cities, railroads, and docks—providing always that the co-operative processes on which modern industry relies are not impaired. But it is just here that the immaterial damage of war is greatest. It wrecks public finances, strains credit and monetary systems, dislocates price and cost relations, and distorts the pattern of specialized employment. Let us make no mistake. The postwar world will not be idyllic. It will be poisoned by civil wars and vindictive hatreds, by currency inflations and unemployment, by broken transport and run-down economic systems, and by starvation and disease. Anyone who dreams of a peaceful and prosperous world immediately this war ends is deluding himself. The best we can hope for is to restrain the worst excesses and cope with the greatest social dangers, while building foundations for a more secure and a happier future. Even these modest tasks will strain all our resources and ingenuity and good will.[1]

They cannot be fulfilled with even moderate success unless we build now the instruments of common action by

[1] Cf. J. B. Condliffe, *Agenda for a Postwar World* (New York: W. W. Norton & Co., 1942).

136

all the United Nations. It is impossible at this time to foresee in detail what action will be necessary; but it is possible to devise flexible machinery, to choose competent administrators and commission them to work out plans to mobilize expert staffs and resources. Such organization takes time, and we may not have much time to prepare for such a gigantic emergency.

The first test of public will is upon us in the United States. No economist believes that the complex disorder of international trading relations can be disentangled by popular debate or political logrolling. The restoration of world trade must be negotiated in technical detail by executive experts. For such negotiations it is essential to renew the President's powers to conclude reciprocal trade agreements. Before June these powers come up for Congressional consideration. Failure to renew them would be construed all over the world as convincing evidence that the United States does not intend to co-operate effectively in a world system after this war. We ought not to allow unpreparedness to bring upon us a repetition of the tragedy that followed the last war.

Given renewal of these powers, the United Nations can proceed to negotiate a restoration of world trade and to buttress that restoration by setting up machinery for currency stabilization, for orderly economic development of backward industrial areas, for systematic disposal of crop surpluses, and for co-ordination of national credit policies.[2] Technicians are in broad agreement upon the essential characteristics of the machinery, but the best machinery will not run without motive power. The motive power

---

[2] Cf. J. B. Condliffe, *Problems of Economic Reorganization* (New York: Commission to Study the Organization of Peace, 1943).

of government is political will, and it is for an informed and resolute public opinion to build that will to action.

This is hardly the occasion to develop in detail the technical methods by which orderly economic collaboration may be developed first among the United Nations and then among all peoples who are ready to co-operate with them. The objectives I have just mentioned—currency stabilization, economic development, commodity regulation, and credit co-ordination—do not exhaust the possibilities of fruitful collaboration in an orderly and peaceful world. They are mentioned as perhaps the most urgent tasks to be tackled when the first urgent relief and medical needs of a war-stricken world have been met. Monetary inflation, disordered commodity markets, and poverty of capital resources will call for determined and rapid action. A long list could be made of other fields where collaboration is urgent, but in the tragic circumstances that will almost certainly confront us when the war ends we should at least be sure of coping with the worst threats of disaster. It may even be necessary to aim first at limited measures —to peg the dollar and sterling together so that other currencies may find in their stability a rock upon which to base themselves, to plan programs for the restoration of essential transport services in vital areas, and to establish effective measures for allocating supplies of a few basic foodstuffs and raw materials.

The important steps to take at the moment are first to establish certain principles of action—the principles of expanding multilateral trade, of stable exchanges, of co-ordinated monetary policies, of consultation in allocating scarce foods and raw materials, and of co-operative effort to get the peoples of the world working again. In order to implement these principles it is necessary to establish organs of collaboration—a United Nations Monetary Organization, a United Nations Commodity Corporation, a United Nations Development Corporation. The plans for such organizations should be worked out; nuclear staffs should be selected and set to work on preparations for action when the time arrives.

There is always a last word to be added. Freedom from want depends upon freedom from fear. No nation will embark upon economic co-operation and interdependence if it fears a renewal of aggression. Peace and prosperity go hand in hand. Prosperity buttresses the hope of peace, but it depends upon effective measures to ensure peace. The hopes of a war-torn world, the aspirations of the young men who are now risking their lives for victory, and the prayers of those who are left at home are fixed upon a lasting peace—a peace that will enable us to build in due time a world of political and economic freedom. If for petty interest or lack of vision we disappoint those hopes and prayers, there will be neither freedom from want nor freedom from fear in our time.

THE LAND AND HUMAN WELFARE

BJARNE BRAATOY

*Chief Intelligence Officer in the Planning Division of the
Office of War Information of the Government of the
United States of America*

IN THE SERIES OF SUBJECTS WE ARE DISCUSSING AT THIS
conference none is more fundamental to an understanding
of the mental climate of our age than the subject of land
and human welfare. To us all land means space. And
space is the prerequisite of human welfare—space that we
can cultivate, space that we can exploit. Nor is any of
the subjects before us more fundamental to our discussion
of the world conflict in which we are engaged. The
aggressor nations are obsessed by the notion of space.
Japan started the struggle for space more than eleven years
ago. Italy followed suit in December, 1934, and Germany
began by moving into Austria in March, 1938.

We are not ourselves free from this obsession. This
nation has grown in the sign of the expanding frontier.
We were lucky to have a largely unpopulated continent
in which to expand. It has saved us from the mania for
space which seems to characterize most nations. But we
have been saved in appearance only. Our expansion within
continental frontiers has not been free from the cruel
aspects with which we tend to reproach the history of
other expansive nations. We have used our dollars to
buy space in Alaska and in the West Indies. And we have

140

only salved our consciences in the Philippines by concessions that have yet to materialize.

We are associated with nations in this war who are even less able than we to repudiate the claim that they are "space maniacs." And there are people among us who have an uneasy feeling that fundamentally we are merely fighting within one imperialistic combine to defeat another.

Our enemies have made it slightly easier for us by being frank about their aims. They are out to gain space, while we are by implication merely defending space that we have already gained. Among our enemies, the Germans have clothed their aims in varying phraseology. They need raw materials. They need breathing space. They want to unite people who belong together "racially." But it always comes down to one fundamental issue, that of space. It does not matter that the Germans have developed their presentation of this issue into a special category in the social sciences. When they talk of geopolitics, teach geopolitics, and equip academic institutes of geopolitics, it is only camouflage for the demand for what they call living space. In my student days in Germany, when geopolitics was only a budding "science," we all recognized that this was just another name for the theory of imperialism.

We might get away from the issue by asserting that our enemies are out for more imperialism while we are out for less imperialism. But I do not think that this dispels our own uneasiness about the fundamental issue. One of the reasons why it does help us is, I think, that the question of space is an obsession within the confines of our national communities as well. Space in terms of land is fundamental to our community feeling. We belong to the land just as much as the land belongs to us. Few of us are many generations away from people who made their living on the land. Even today sixty per cent of the population of this earth belongs to the land. In spite of everything we see and experience in this age of industrialization, our standards remain those of the countryman. His standards are healthy and natural. Industrial civilization is unhealthy.

This uneasiness is both conscious and unconscious. In any case it represents a general recognition of the lack of integration of the modern community. Between the two world wars the uneasiness grew both nationally and internationally, because the mechanisms of an industrial civilization proved unable to serve the interests of the people of the land. The uneasiness turned into a global bad conscience as the cities and industrial centers encroached upon the land and the interests of the land without satisfying the people of the land and without adequate co-ordination. The operations of finance, the provision of tools, marketing arrangements, and even health services and education seemed increasingly to become a prerogative of the city dweller, or at least to be concentrated in the cities. The people with space did not benefit from their possession of this space, and the people who apparently despoiled them did so with a bad conscience.

This uneasiness and the victims of the circumstances which stimulated this uneasiness gave what we call Fascism its chance. The people who migrated from the land to the cities and industrial centers were the recruits of Fascist movements all over the world. As industrialism developed, it spread to the countryside in the shape of a mechanized agriculture which in its turn barred the way back to the migrants when farming began to regain some measure of prosperity. In all countries the idea that the scourge of our civilization, mass unemployment, could

142

be healed by means of a prosperous agriculture was frustrated by the facts of mechanized agriculture.

Fascism exploited the consequent dilemma, nationally to secure recruits, and internationally to make a case for its claims. There is one outstanding example of the failure of Fascism to succeed in this endeavor, and one outstanding example of its success.

The example of its failure that I want to place before you is Sweden. During the twenties Sweden developed her industries on a scale and at a pace unknown to history. Politically and socially the movement of the industrial workers in Sweden forged ahead apace with this development. At the same time Swedish agriculture was passing through the most difficult period in its history. Politically and socially, if not also economically, the uneasiness of which I have spoken threatened to develop into a profound division in the national community with labor on one side and the farmers on the other. I am leaving aside here the traditional analysis of a capitalist civilization with the capitalists opposed to the workers. One reason is that the farmers developed anticapitalist trends in the process. It was in a wider sense a split between the countryside and the cities.

Matters came to a head during the early thirties when the world economic crisis hit Sweden. At that time the farmers organized in every sense for a battle with organized labor. This development coincided with the rise of Hitlerism. From across the Baltic came slogans that might have succeeded in transforming the people of the Swedish countryside into the banner bearers of Fascism— or of Nazidom, if you like. In 1933 and early 1934 it was touch and go whether the contagion should spread on a scale sufficient to engulf Sweden.

It did not happen. And I would like to outline briefly

the main reasons why it did not happen. I shall spare you the psychological arguments. We shall leave aside the nature of the Swedish people. We shall ignore the democratic traditions of Sweden and deal simply with the practical measures developed by the Swedish people to handle the problem of the land and human welfare.

The critical year was 1932. The number of bankruptcies and forced sales of farms was reaching an all-time high. Unemployment in industry was also increasing on a serious scale. But the menace came from conditions on the land. Generally speaking, the Swedes were as uncertain about the remedy as the peoples of other countries. They were certainly as disunited. The farmers spoke for themselves; the financiers and industrialists were concerned with their own plight; and traditionally the movement of the industrial workers was expected to think only in terms of what could be done to remedy industrial unemployment.

Into this confusion came a plan for a new deal for Sweden. The plan came from the political party of Swedish labor, the Social Democrats. The surprising thing about this plan was the emphasis it laid on conditions on the land. In March, 1932, the Swedish Parliament was faced with an elaborate plan of measures to alleviate the crisis for the distressed sections of the population, "the unemployed workers and the poverty-stricken farmers, threatened with bankruptcy." The plan tied them together and illustrated specifically that one could not be helped without the other.

In the parliamentary elections in the fall the farming population of Sweden was still opposed to the industrial population, but during the winter of 1932 to 1933 they got together. The organizing ability of the Swedish industrial worker, proved in the trade unions and the co-

144

operatives of Sweden, was brought to bear on the problems of the land. A solidarity in fact and not only in principle was displayed. It was recognized that the industrial worker could not expect his living conditions to improve independently of the improvement of living conditions on the land, and in 1936 the Farmers' Party of Sweden joined hands with the workers' party of Sweden in government. For ten years now Sweden has shown that a fundamental cleavage in the modern community can be healed by an organized, rational approach. I would even go further and say that Sweden has shown how an industrial civilization can become healthy and harmonious.

In Germany the solution was sought and accepted by strong-arm methods. Indeed, the outcome indicates that no solution was sought. The uneasiness and bad conscience of the community as a whole was exploited by a back-to-nature movement which camouflaged the lust for power of a small group, the original Nazis, and the egoism of a group of industrialists and financiers. They financed the appeal which brought an increasing stream of volunteers from the countryside to the Nazi movement. A considerable part of the political leverage was provided by the big landowners. You may say that without the cleavage between the people of the land and the people of the industrial centers Hitler could not have succeeded. You may explain his success also by the federal structure of Germany at the time which did not allow a centralized plan like the Swedish one to take roots. You may explain it by other elements in the situation—the particularly disastrous effects of the world economic crisis in Germany, the lack of unity in the labor movement in Germany, the financial and economic ostracism which Germany suffered during the years of immediate economic world crisis from 1929 to 1933. But the effects of internal developments were in the main conditioned by the fundamental cleavage between the land and the town.

The appeal to the supposed victim of this cleavage went beyond the frontiers of Germany. In the first place, the cleavage was not restricted to Germany. It existed even in Europe's most peaceful corner, Scandinavia. It was present throughout the whole of Eastern and Southeastern Europe, where the first World War had brought ownership of land to the peasants but not stability and peace of mind. In the second place, the cleavage was accentuated throughout these lands and the appeal of Hitler's back-to-nature philosophy given greater potency by the existence of a German-speaking element on the land in Poland, in Czechoslovakia, in Hungary, and in Roumania. Where the appeal to the people of the land did not succeed in itself, the appeal to people of a kindred tongue might carry.

Nazidom exploited a further element in one situation which existed independently of the rise of Hitlerism. Europe had become unbalanced not only in terms of the land and human welfare but also in terms of possible solutions. In this connection the solution which had been sought and found in the Soviet Union only added to the confusion. There the cleavage had been healed—or an attempt to heal it had been made—by means of organizing agriculture along the same lines as Soviet industry. To the peasants and farmers of Eastern Europe, indeed to the farmers of all the rest of Europe, this solution was not acceptable. The farmers of the countries along the western border of Russia had recently just become owners of their land or were fighting for an organization of agriculture that would make them owners of their land. To them the solution was the Scandinavian one of producer co-operatives and not imposed collectivization of the land. The Nazis were

146

able to exploit this aversion to the Soviet solution in terms of the cleavage already existing in the Central and Eastern European countries. The farm population did not like the industrial population. The latter was said to be imbued with Communist doctrines which would impose upon the farming population an alien system. This proves that the proposed Nazi and Fascist solution was no solution of the split personality of the national communities in Europe. It only aggravated the condition.

Before the two wars, an outlet for frustrations and apparently insoluble situations had been provided for the peoples of Europe by the existence of a hospitable land over here. If things got too bad on the land in Europe, you could always escape to the free and open spaces in North America. It was an escape and not a solution, but it did help to prevent the evolution of a situation such as broke in on Europe during the thirties. But we have been increasingly unwilling to receive people from overseas, and in the twenties we also started to seal the entry against goods from overseas.

We became a protectionist country in stages. The decisive indication of how far we were prepared to go in protecting ourselves came in 1928. I was living in Central Europe at that time. I wonder whether any of you realize what an impression it made on the peoples of that area when they learned that these United States were raising a tariff barrier that might cut Europe off from trade with these shores. It does not matter whether we ultimately went that far or not. The impression was created, and it was grist to the mill of Fascism. Europe became open to the arguments of the maniacs for space, space at home and space abroad. European neoimperialism was nourished by American protectionism. It is no coincidence that the last statesman of democratic Germany whose name had weight internationally, Foreign Minister Stresemann, and the representative of Italy, Scialoja, used the 1929 Assembly of the League of Nations to warn the world of the consequences if the problems of raw materials and access to markets and space were not solved in an organized way.

It was no longer an exclusively European problem. It was not even primarily a European problem. Faced with a rising tide of protectionism, Japan turned maniac and broke into Manchuria in September, 1931. The demand for space turned up with a vengeance. We did not tackle the problem of land and human welfare internationally. We went on the defensive. The Dominions demanded a system of imperial preferences in their trade relations with Britain. Trade barriers went up in one country after the other, thus only adding fuel to the fire of the rising clamor for space.

It is curious and valuable to note that this clamor arose in nations where training in democratic procedure was not of long standing. The self-discipline and perspective which that training gives had not become part and parcel of the conventions of the community in Japan, Italy, and Germany. Developments showed that the arguments advanced for their subsequent aggressive action were in reality mere arguments. Japan did not utilize the space that she conquered in Manchuria to give room to a surplus population from the homeland. The number of people that Italy transferred to her overseas empire was too small to count. Germany's first chance to transfer populations in Europe was used to bring back from the Baltic State German-speaking families who had been settled there for generations. She made an agreement with Italy to bring back into German-speaking areas people from the Italian Tyrol who had also been settled there for generations.

And the war has made it necessary for Germany to use more than six million foreigners on her own soil, beside transferring foreigners from one part of occupied territory to another. The space myth has been exploded by events engineered by the very people who were most eager to advance the myth.

And as far as raw materials are concerned, even a protectionist world proved able to provide the three space-maniac nations with materials for war on a scale that we are only beginning to realize. Where there was a will there evidently was a way for Japan and for Germany, if not quite to a comparable extent for Italy.

If the will that was undeniably present had been devoted to the end of human welfare, possibly the problem of space could have been solved without eleven years of continuous and expanding misery for untold millions. But it could not have been solved by any nation on its own and for itself. During the years between the two wars this was on the whole recognized by most nations. The League of Nations was a symbol of this recognition, but we have to take into account two things in this connection. The first was the absence of our own country throughout those twenty years. The second was the limited authority of the League in financial and economic matters. For the problems that concern us here it had practically no authority and no machinery. The financial and economic sections of the League were in the main research centers with limited funds and limited personnel. The International Institute of Agriculture in Rome was similarly limited in authority and capacity.

The mechanism of international co-operation therefore became the old-fashioned conference. During the century preceding the first World War the conference had evolved as a startling and increasingly democratic instrument of international co-operation. By the time the first World War was over, however, it was generally realized that conferences do not in themselves constitute a mechanism of operation. You need the continuous services of a secretariat, regular meetings, and the development of rules and authority. The treaty makers of 1919 failed to bring this maxim into the treaties in the field of economic affairs. And so the world found its main problems dealt with in a haphazard and disjointed fashion by occasional international conferences, of which the most important were held in Genoa in 1922, in Geneva in 1927, and in London in 1933.

The first two conferences were handicapped in the same way as our delegates to the peace conferences. The governments did not possess authority in economic and financial matters. The second of the two conferences did not even pretend to possess governmental authority. It was a conference of experts delegated by governments and private organizations. The third, the one in London in 1933, was held after the world economic crisis had brought a turning of the tide in regard to governmental authority in financial and economic matters, but too early for that authority to get firmly into the saddle so that agreements would make sense both in execution and on paper. None of them was therefore capable of handling problems of international economic organization in such a way as to take the edge off the space argument.

There was nevertheless a distinct change in the mental climate of those handling these problems between the era of the twenties and that of the thirties. In the twenties the idea had in the main been to confer with a view to paving the way for agreements between private organizations. In the thirties it was realized that private international agreements in matters of material concern to the peoples of the world were not adequate. The agreements

150

needed government backing. As the governments had in the meantime been acquiring authority and experience in economic affairs, it proved possible to conclude a series of commodity agreements with the stability in production and marketing arrangements which governments could assure to a greater extent than private organizations, at least internationally. The demands of Stresemann and Scialoja at the 1929 Assembly of the League of Nations were in fact being met, but too late to stem the rising tide of Fascism and aggression.

These commodity agreements of the midthirties were handicapped in one essential respect which was and remains of the most decisive importance to the people of the land. The bookkeeping arrangements between the nations, international finance, must have a stable unit and a mechanism to ensure that stability if the people of the land are to regain their assurance and the communities of the world are to find a balanced outlook. That is where these United States finally moved in and helped. In 1936 an agreement was concluded with Britain and France which in fact served to stabilize monetary arrangements. It embraced the sterling bloc. The remaining gold-standard countries came in. Only Germany refused to join. But the principle and the mechanism had been established. One of the great discoveries in international affairs had been made. Nobody knows how much trouble the agreement spared the world in the brief period left before the war broke out in Europe and finally engulfed the world. Very few people realize how fruitful the development was which this government helped to seal. It is the cornerstone of the international arrangements which will make the clamor for space, for land, internationally less troublesome after this war than it has ever been. Whether you call the mechanism an international monetary authority, an inter-

151

national bank, or international co-operation between exchange controls does not matter. It has been proved that human ingenuity can find the way to a mechanism of stability in relations between national economies.

Before this discovery—or, if you like, invention—had been made, a relative stability had been secured within the sterling bloc centralized in London. This was the external guarantee of that solution which Sweden found to our problem. Internal bookkeeping in Sweden's new deal was not endangered by instability in the unit of Sweden's external bookkeeping, once Sweden had devalued in accordance with the pound sterling. But the burden was proving too heavy for London, and it may be that the Washington-London-Paris agreement saved Sweden's new deal in the spring of 1937 when Sweden's foreign exchange rate was in danger for the one and only time.

Between the nations operating these new-style agreements and mechanisms for the control of international monetary relations and commodity markets, space was no longer a burning problem in the old and primitive sense. The possession of areas producing specific raw materials was of less consequence when their exploitation was a matter for orderly and authoritative handling between the nations concerned, just as the conflict between the people of the land and those of the industrial centers became less acute as machinery for orderly marketing and co-ordination of social benefits came into the hands of the government within the national community with the free and willing co-operation of the sections concerned. The quest for security and stability does not end at that point, because factors beyond normal control always arise, and mechanisms are never perfect; but the uneasiness of the civilization that we have known, the deep-rooted disaffection that is expressed in contrary values and standards, may be overcome where a common meeting ground is found for handling the problems involved. If we control the governments and the governments have the machinery for handling our crucial problems nationally and internationally, the rest is education.

But a great war has intervened between the picture I have tried to sketch and problems even more vast than those we had begun to handle in an orderly way so far as democratic authority and interests could reach. We shall not be faced with the problem merely of adjusting differences of existence and outlook, but of alleviating untold distress and filling bottomless needs. The land will indeed be called upon to contribute to human welfare when we face the period of postwar relief and rehabilitation. We cannot afford to disappoint once again peoples who have heard our promises, this time of the four freedoms, the third of which is freedom from want. I am sure that we do not desire to disappoint them, if only because the disappointment would inevitably recoil upon ourselves.

I have tried to sketch a background of our traditions and aptitudes for handling a problem of the kind. I have tried to suggest that the peoples of the world are hardly emerging from a self-centered obsession with space. I have submitted that the solutions for the problems of the land and human welfare are no longer primarily to be found on the land, but in the development of organized mechanisms for handling the relations between the land and human welfare, internationally as well as nationally. I shall now for a moment forget all that and try to consider the postwar problem in as immediate and straightforward a manner as possible.

Where do we start? I should think that we start with an estimate of the prospective needs that we shall be called upon to fill. What will the debilitated peoples in disrupted communities throughout devastated areas actually need— in food, in clothing, in fuel, in medical supplies and services, in equipment to help them to begin again if only in the most primitive fashion?

How can we find out? After all, the main body of sufferers are out of our reach. They are under enemy occupation in Europe and in the Far East. We do not know where they are, how many they are, in what condition they are. And even if we knew today, we could not be certain that our facts would hold good when relief can start.

Are we the people to find out? Have we in America the experts to devote to the task of finding the facts, analyzing them, and drawing reasonably reliable deductions from them? These United States may be a melting pot of people hailing from all the areas in question. Nevertheless we, their descendants, do not for that reason possess the expert qualifications necessary to estimate conditions in foreign lands.

We do not, fortunately, have to go further in speculation; for the work in question has started, and answers, at least partial ones, are being provided. Finding the facts from which prospective needs may be estimated has been going on in relation to every occupied territory practically ever since the territory in question became occupied. The governments-in-exile all considered that job as a main responsibility. Keeping in touch with the people in the occupied territory, they could not avoid receiving reports of conditions, of the looting by the enemy, of production and needs. They could not even if they wanted to. Apart from their immediate interest in the matter, this job was necessary for the prosecution of the war. And nobody could be better qualified for the job than the authorities coming from the territories in question themselves. They know the situation from before the war. They know the language, the methods of finding and estimating facts of the people at home; they know the people providing the reports. They may not enjoy unanimous confidence among the people at home, any more than any government does, war or no war, but they at least enjoy greater confidence than any foreign authority. So the governments-in-exile have been accumulating facts that will allow us to estimate the needs of the occupied nations, and to revise our estimates as conditions change.

These reports and estimates on needs cannot be based on the assumption that all you have to do is to ask and you will receive. Even if the supplies were there, the question of adequate transport would come in. And we have to think in terms of supplies to areas stretching from Norway to the Philippines and China. And supplies just will not be there. The needs undoubtedly will be too great for the supplies available at the end of the war, whether it ends at once everywhere or in stages from one area to another.

The governments concerned realized this and got together in a meeting in London in September, 1941. It was the meeting in which the Allies subscribed to the Atlantic Charter. But the importance of the meeting went far beyond the terms of the Atlantic Charter. The Allies, including the Soviet Union, agreed, in the first place, to cooperate in finding out the prospective relief needs of their territories. They agreed, in the second place, to pool whatever supplies might be available so as to effect an equitable distribution. They agreed, in the third place, to pool the means of transportation, above all shipping. And, finally, they agreed to the establishment of a mechanism for dealing with the problem, the Inter-Allied Post-War Requirements Bureau in London.

In principle this answers all the questions we asked above. But there is a lot of detail to be filled in. And an office working in London in wartime conditions may not be able to fill in all the details. Certain elements of the problems are being handled elsewhere, particularly by the remnants of the League of Nations machinery on this side of the Atlantic, the International Labor Office in Montreal and the economic and financial sections of the League Secretariat in Princeton. Last November this government appointed officials for the task of dealing with this problem. The Office of Relief and Rehabilitation is already trying its hand at the job in North Africa, and is undoubtedly developing means of participation in the London mechanism, which was established before the United States came into the war. In itself it is evidence of the realization that an international mechanism does not absolve the national governments from working on a problem. On the contrary, it presupposes their contributory work.

I should like to be slightly more specific about the work that is being done. I have had the opportunity to study one report from, or rather to, a government-in-exile on the prospective needs of its territory. It started with a map of a slice of territory on the coast of Europe somewhere. It included population figures, prewar, and population estimates on the basis of war losses, increasing death rate, forced transfer of labor. It went into detail about harbor and transport facilities. And it established a plan for seaborne deliveries which would permit practically simultaneous delivery starting, say, in South America on a given date, in Canada on another given earlier date, and in Britain on a still earlier date, to all sections of the area. The work has in other words progressed so far that not only have definite needs been estimated in regard to certain areas, but the transport and administrative aspects have been taken in hand.

If I were to detail the specific needs and supplies that

were brought out in the above report, I would be giving away the source. That cannot be done because these reports are, as I said, of importance for the prosecution of the war as well as for the relief period. It will be clear to you all that clothing is one of the essential needs everywhere. But clothing includes shoes and outdoor clothing. The specifications would allow you to deduce whether the report, and in consequence the conditions described, related, say, to Greece, to Holland, or to Arctic Norway. As long as the war goes on there will, therefore, be strict limits to the scope of public discussion of these matters. The correctives of a critical public opinion can apply less to the appreciation of actual material needs and the satisfaction of those needs than to the machinery for handling the problem. This consideration places democratic control in a difficult position. The problem appeals to us because of its substance, crying human needs of specific kinds, and the possibilities that we have of delivering the goods. The framework is less appealing, except when personalities are involved, and then it is largely occasional, if not negative. The mechanisms of the framework lie beyond the experience and possible intelligent interest of most of us, certainly as soon as it becomes international and is no longer merely of national concern.

This explains why so little is known about the wartime developments in this sphere. It also helps to explain why the results up to date are not what they should be. Of course everybody involved in this work has, at the same time, been involved in total war; and there is a lack of manpower for this type of specialized work, just as we are realizing the lack of manpower relative to the claims of the war in all fields. But a new impetus to public interest has been given by the appointment of an official to direct the American end, former Governor

Lehman, who is in the public eye and who commands public attention in his own right. We are all increasingly aware of the obligations of the United Nations in this respect and shall expect to hear constant reports of progress in the preparatory work. In this manner the corrective of public opinion is being brought to bear internationally as well as in the underground relations between the occupied nations and their authorities in exile. These obligations have been made part of our consciousness not merely by means of the promises expressed in one United Nations declaration after the other, in our propaganda to Allied, occupied, and enemy territories, and in statements by our leaders, but also in the legislation and reports from the President that have accompanied the development of our lend-lease policy. Relief is becoming part of our conventional morality, or our moral conventions, if you like. I am using this term in a strictly objective sense on the assumption that you will all agree to the compelling force of that element in the working of our communities.

So far we have in the main only established the framework of the job. We are trying to implement it and to gain some experience in execution in North Africa. In regard to one commodity, wheat, a pool was agreed upon between the five main wheat-exporting nations, but even that is only a beginning.

In dealing with the problem of the land and human welfare I have tried to show you the contradictions between our traditional conceptions and the means which a modern, mechanized, and industrialized civilization makes necessary. I have also tried to show you that democracy has proved its ability to devise fruitful means of solving those contradictions, both nationally and internationally. And, finally, I hope that I have convinced you of the continuity of democratic effort in this field, to justify the range of my discussion, from land in the most immediate and material sense to human welfare in a comprehensive and global sense.

BIBLIOGRAPHY

Neumann, S.: "Fashions in Space." *Foreign Affairs*, January, 1943.

Will, Ed: "I Speak for the Middle-Class Farmer." *The Saturday Evening Post*, January 30, 1943.

Royal Institute of International Affairs: *World Agriculture*. New York: Oxford University Press, 1932.

Braatoy, Bjarne: *The New Sweden*. New York: Thomas Nelson & Sons, 1939.

Neumann, Franz: *Behemoth: The Structure and Practice of National Socialism*. New York: Oxford University Press, 1942.

Annual Surveys. Royal Institute of International Affairs, London.

Francis, E. V.: *The Battle for Supplies*. New York: Thomas Nelson & Sons, 1942.

Condliffe, J. B.: *The Reconstruction of World Trade*. New York: W. W. Norton & Co., 1940. With comprehensive bibliography.

"Commodity Control Schemes." *Planning* (London), July, 1941.

Inter-Allied Review, October, 1941. Inter-Allied Information Center, New York.

Reveille, Thomas: *The Spoil of Europe*. New York: W. W. Norton & Co., 1941.

War and Peace Aims. New York: United Nations Information Office, January 30, 1943.

Wild, Payson S., Jr.: "Machinery of Collaboration Between the United Nations." *Foreign Policy Reports*, July 1, 1942.

Schwarz, Sanford: *Research in International Economics by Federal Agencies*. New York: Columbia University Press, 1941.

Fowler, Bertram B.: *Food: A Weapon for Victory*. Boston: Little, Brown & Co., 1942.

Motherwell, Hiram: "The Strategy of Feeding Europe." *Harper's Magazine*, January, 1943.

McDougall, E. L.: "International Aspects of Postwar Food and Agriculture." *Annals of the American Academy of Political and Social Science*, January, 1943.

Marshall, C. B.: "The Lend-Lease Operation." *Ibid.*

Relief for Europe. Washington: National Planning Association.

munity in which he lives. This attitude toward the human being, without which the world would be merely the kind of "nasty and brutish" shambles described by Hobbes, is present in all religious beliefs, and can be displayed by monarchies as well as by republics, by peoples regarded as backward as well as by the most technically developed peoples. Any society that treats the human being as a mere inanimate object—whether as a cog in the industrial machine or as cannon fodder in the armed forces—is by definition antidemocratic, no matter how many elections it may hold, or how many kinds of freedom it may offer its citizens on paper. By contrast, any society in which human beings treat each other with respect for their individual qualities and concern for their individual weaknesses comes within the definition of democracy, no matter how little it may possess of the political machinery which in the past we have too often regarded as synonymous with the democratic way of life. And just as within each nation that claims to be democratic we must strive to give room for the development of individuals of the most varied origins and equipped with the most varied skills and talents, so in the international community we must strive to give an opportunity for the unhampered development of the many national groups that make up the world —provided they, in turn, discharge their share of responsibility for the maintenance and improvement of international society.

Our political aim, during the war and after, should be not only unity, but diversity within unity. No valid approach can be made to the problems of political reconstruction in Europe and Asia without understanding at the outset that no single formula is applicable to every nation or area of these continents, since all of them are, in a sense, living in different periods of history.

Before the war some of the European countries—Britain, France, Holland, Belgium, and the Scandinavian nations—had already emerged into the twentieth century. Their pioneering political, economic, and social achievements had profoundly affected the countries of the New World, from whom, in turn, they had borrowed new techniques, especially in the industrial field. Germany, which gave the appearance of having emerged into the twentieth century because it utilized the modern techniques of industry and warfare more effectively than Britain and France, had not shared in the political transformations that have shaped Western civilization. Meanwhile, Russia and its neighbors in Eastern Europe and the Balkans are, with varying degrees of rapidity, telescoping the social and economic revolutions of the past two centuries into a brief span of years. And in the Far East the distance—not in space but in history—between the various countries of that region may be measured by the wide gaps that separate China, which is just achieving a sense of national unity, India, where nationalism is reaching the boiling point, and colonial areas like the Malay States and the Dutch East Indies, which were just beginning to feel the impact of modern nationalism before the Japanese invasion.

The political convulsions that are taking place throughout the world are further complicated by the desperate efforts of national groups, some of which have been forced for long periods of time to live under alien rule, to achieve at one and the same time national independence and economic progress. What Europe and Asia need most of all is to be roughly equalized, so that the various peoples who inhabit these continents can act out of a more or less common experience for a more or less common purpose. The war has speeded up this process of equalization, and has united Europeans and Asiatics, at least superficially—

but united them *against* the Nazi or Japanese "new order," not yet always *for* a joint endeavor of reconstruction. To effect such unity in an affirmative, and no longer a negative, sense is one of the tasks that challenges the statesmanship of the United Nations.

Just as the political landscape is changing rapidly before our eyes, so the economic structure with which we are familiar is beginning to show many cracks and fissures. The wartime experience of Britain, Russia, and the United States, as well as Germany and Japan, demonstrates that industrial production has practically no bounds when a supreme effort is required for national survival. Once hostilities are over, it will be very difficult to persuade workers who may be thrown out of employment as a result of demobilization of war industries that there is any technical obstacle to peacetime continuance of production on the same scale as that achieved in time of war. We may therefore expect a demand on the part of demobilized soldiers and workers that the state, if necessary, should intervene to provide them with opportunities for work. Nor will men and women who were so urgently needed in time of war, and have had the uplifting experience of utilizing their skills and talents to the utmost, be satisfied to accept some kind of dole or relief from the state in lieu for creative activity. For they will also have learned that economic forces are not uncontrollable like the forces of nature but on the contrary can be controlled by human beings and harnessed to tasks regarded as necessary for the welfare of the community, provided the will to do so exists. They will bring to postwar reconstruction a spirit combining faith in the capacity and initiative of the individual with belief in the need to pool individual efforts for the benefit of the community as a whole.

While this profound readjustment is taking place in the

165

relation of the individual to the society in which he lives, equally profound changes are taking place in the economy of all nations. Countries like Britain which since the early days of the Industrial Revolution had concentrated on the production of manufactured goods, exporting them overseas in return for foodstuffs and raw materials, have found under pressure of war that they had to expand their agriculture to avoid the danger of starvation. Meanwhile, many of the countries which had previously produced and exported foodstuffs and raw materials to the advanced industrial powers—China, India, the nations of Latin America—also under pressure of war are establishing industries which can supply them, if not with machinery and manufactured goods requiring mass production, at least with consumers' goods they once imported.

These changes, which in turn hasten the process of equalizing economic, and ultimately political, conditions throughout the world, may well persist into the postwar world. If they do, it may mean that Britain and the United States, for example, will no longer find markets abroad for certain consumers' goods—such as textiles or shoes—and may have to readapt the production of factories manufacturing such goods for distribution primarily in their own domestic markets. Such a change in the channels of distribution promises to result in a rise, and not a decline, in our own standard of living. At the same time we may find that, as the standard of living rises in newly industrialized countries, these countries will provide a far larger market than in the past for the products of British and American heavy industries, such as tools, machinery, automobiles, airplanes, railway equipment, and so on. Moreover, the increasing use of synthetic materials—synthetic rubber and oil, as well as plastics—will place at the disposal of countries which lack natural raw materials the

166

possibility of providing themselves with some of the resources needed for modern industry. If these developments take place, then the economic emphasis after the war may be far less on "access to raw materials," as stated in the Atlantic Charter, than on "access" to the inventions of scientists, which should be made freely available to all countries.

This does not mean that all international trade will vanish after the war, but it may mean that it will no longer be based on the orthodox economic principle of "division of labor" among various nations supposed to be freely exchanging their products. This principle, as a matter of fact, rationalized the inequality that existed in the nineteenth century, and in some regions persists in our own times, between the industrial and agricultural areas of the world. Division of labor implied, in part, that the Western peoples, who had been the first to learn modern industrial techniques, would remain indefinitely in a superior position, manufacturing finished and semi-finished goods for their own use and for export, while the peoples of backward regions would, also indefinitely, perform the less complicated and more menial tasks of raising crops and mining ores for export to industrialized countries.

This situation, if unchanged, spelled continuance of a low standard of living in the so-called backward areas which, because of their backwardness, proved to be highly vulnerable to political, military, and economic pressures from their more advanced neighbors or rulers, as we have seen during the past quarter of a century in Europe and Asia. In the long run, this division of labor also blocked the further progress of the industrialized states, which found they had reached a saturation point in trying to sell expensive manufactured goods to peoples living at a low standard of living. Moreover, the discontent generated by the persistence of substandard economic and social conditions in backward countries furnished ready ammunition to Axis propagandists, who tried to convince these peoples that they were an international proletariat oppressed by the "plutocracies" of Britain and the United States. In a sense our industrial achievements proved a boomerang, since the more we publicized our own material progress, the more others, less fortunate than we because of a variety of historical, political, and economic circumstances, began to say: "If the Americans—or the British—can have all these comforts and luxuries, why can't we? Why shouldn't we use our resources to improve our own way of life, instead of making things easy for others, who show no concern in our welfare?" And the tragic paradox was that by no means all of the people in Britain and the United States enjoyed the comforts and luxuries, or even the simple amenities, of life envied by less industrially advanced countries; that many, relatively speaking, would have benefited just as much as the Chinese coolie, or the Russian peasant, or the Indian peon, by having easier access to the products of their own factories and farms.

It would, of course, be still possible for the United States, and Britain, and other nations who have hitherto had a controlling interest in the trade and investments of backward areas, to resist the tendency toward industrialization, in which nationalism is combined with a desire for an improved way of life—resist it, if necessary, by force. But to do this would be to repeat the mistakes of the French and Russian revolutions. It would be to express, in a different form, Marie Antoinette's fateful phrase: "Let them eat cake!" Even if we did use force to prevent the industrialization of Eastern Europe, the Balkans, Latin America, and Asia, we would not be able, ultimately, to stem the tide. Sooner or later we would be engulfed by it, as the French aristocrats and monarchy, and the Russian aristocrats and monarchy, were engulfed in revolution after having refused to effect much-needed reforms. It is impossible to turn back the clock set whirring by the Industrial Revolution. Far better to accept facts as they are graciously, instead of being grudging about it, and voluntarily offer our technical and financial aid in helping other peoples to raise their standard of living and, by the same token, create conditions of literacy and stability which may permit their gradual transition to political conditions approximating democracy. Nothing could be more unrealistic than to expect the backward peoples of the world to adopt democratic practices and at the same time block their efforts to obtain the material tools they need for their own advancement.

The readjustments that are taking place during the war —and may be expected to take place after—in both national and international economy require some degree of planning by mutual consent among the peoples of the world if they are not to result in sheer anarchy. In time of war the need for survival has caused the United Nations to accept far-reaching controls over the use of manpower, as well as the production and distribution of foodstuffs, raw materials, manufactured goods, and shipping. Is it impossible to believe that when the war is over we may accept similar if less drastic controls in order to assure our survival in time of reconstruction? Yet the experience of World War I is not encouraging in this respect. At that time the Allies, confronted with imminent disaster, did pool their resources and, at the eleventh hour, even their armed forces to win the war. But the moment the Armistice was signed this elaborate machinery of international collaboration forged at so great a cost in lives

169

and material was demobilized practically overnight. And instead of utilizing the experience of wartime co-operation for the needs of the postwar period the Allies attempted to create out of whole cloth an international organization—the League of Nations— which had no roots in the experience of the war-weary peoples who had just laid down their arms. It should be our endeavor to see to it that after this war the machinery of international collaboration worked out in Washington, London, Moscow, and Chungking is not demobilized but instead is remobilized and adapted to the tasks of postwar reconstruction.

Yet any attempt at planning, national or international, implies some degree of regulation and control; and this frightens many people who believe that planning will result in totalitarianism, the disappearance of private initiative and enterprise, and the end of democracy. The assumption of those who express this fear is that what we know as capitalism—the system under which private individuals can accumulate capital and invest it in private enterprise—is synonymous with democracy, and is the only system which permits free play for individual initiative.

The capitalist system has proved effective during a period of more than a century which has witnessed the development of new areas of the world, the growth of industry, the expansion of science, the improvement of standards of living in many countries. Today the question is not whether the capitalist system was or was not good in the nineteenth century or even during the early decades of the twentieth, but whether it is undergoing transformations which may hold the promise of even greater social and economic advancement for the world in the future. In the days when private individuals took the risk of investing their capital in new enterprises—railways, public utilities, untried industries, shipping—thus creating new

170

opportunities for employment, the system of private enterprise justified its existence, even if it was often accompanied by such evils as slums, long working hours, low wages, and insufficient facilities for education, leisure, and decent living for large sections of the population.

But when owners of capital became less concerned with the development of new enterprises than with the maintenance of those already in existence, the resulting stagnation in economic life caused people to reconsider the basic assumptions of the prevailing system. We began to realize that economic activity had come to a standstill, not because there was no possibility of further growth, but because such possibilities as existed—for example, developments like the TVA—did not hold out the prospect of the kind of gains that investors, rightly or wrongly, had come to regard as the yardstick of investment. The question then arose whether it might not be more beneficial for the community as a whole—even if less beneficial for some individuals—that the wealth of the nation, to which all contribute in one way or another, should be devoted first of all to enterprises that would be productive of advantages for the nation as a whole. The yardstick by which decisions regarding future economic development should be measured was no longer that of financial gain but of benefit to the community—although that might mean that all members of the community, in varying degree, might get less cash for their personal use.

The economic relationship of the individual to the community is bound to assume increasing importance as more and more countries become industrialized. For in the industrial society, in contrast to the rural society of pre–Industrial Revolution days, the individual who meets with illness or accident, or loses his job, cannot usually rely on himself, or his family, or the aid of his neighbors.

171

As a worker or employee in a large industrial enterprise, his employment depends not merely on his own ability or conscientiousness but on many factors over which he, as an individual, has no control. He may be willing to work, and to use part of his wages for some form of insurance, but this is usually not enough to assure him of subsistence in case of illness, accident, or prolonged unemployment. The modern industrial system, with its carefully co-ordinated operations and assembly lines, must have as its social counterpart a system of mutual assistance for those who, most often through no fault of their own, are forced to drop out of it from time to time—a system to which not only the worker and employer, but also the community as a whole, in the form of taxes, contributes its share. And just as in the national economy we need this pooling of efforts to assist each other over the rough spots of life, so in the international community we must learn to pool our efforts to give all nations—not only the strong great powers—a modicum of political security and economic stability.

This reconsideration of economic assumptions which was going on before the war has been greatly speeded up in all countries by the war itself. Today the national wealth of the United States, in the form of taxes, savings, purchases of war bonds, and so on, is being used by the nation, as represented by the government, to produce armaments, maintain armed forces, and prosecute the war. It is estimated that by the time the war is over the United States government will be the sole buyer of from sixty to seventy per cent of the entire national output, and will have more than thirty million citizens on its payroll. We accept this far-reaching control by the government over the nation's economic life because we think it is necessary for our common welfare. Might

172

it not happen that we shall accept similar controls after the war for the same reason—because we may come to think that welfare is best served by pooling our resources, instead of having individuals decide just how they will invest their funds?

This does not mean that private property, private enterprise, or private initiative are doomed. Today the government maps out the main lines of production, both in industry and in agriculture, and leaves it to industrial managers, workers, and farmers to carry out these general directives. It would be difficult to prove that the managers and workers who have co-operated, for example, in the conversion of automobile plants to the production of airplanes have been prevented from displaying enterprise and initiative. On the contrary, they have seldom been so challenged to use every ounce of energy, ingenuity, and skill that they possess.

Nor is there any reason to believe that private personal property—as distinguished from private capital—will necessarily vanish in a more or less controlled economy. The Soviet government, which has gone further than any other in restricting private enterprise, has developed a system which can be described as anticapitalist but not anti-private-property. In the U.S.S.R. the individual can own as much private personal property as he finds it possible to buy—such as books, furniture, domestic utensils, clothes, a house in the country, an automobile if he can get one. His possibilities of owning this kind of property are limited only by the fact that during the past quarter of a century Soviet industry has been devoted chiefly to the production of machinery and armaments and not consumers' goods. What the Russian cannot do is accumulate his wages or other earnings and then invest them in a private enterprise where he would employ workers under his personal control. As the war goes on, we may find that similar conditions appear in this country. We all have the right, legally speaking, to own tires, but because of war necessities we cannot buy them. Unlike the Russians, we still have the right to accumulate capital for investment in private enterprise, but more and more of our excess funds will be taken by the government, through taxation or purchase of war bonds, and applied to the needs of war production.

Once the war is over, if we can work out ways and means to live in anticipation of peace and not, as we have been living since 1914, in constant anticipation of war, there is bound to be in Russia, as in the United States, a vast increase in the production of consumers' goods to satisfy the delayed, or never satisfied, demands of the population. When that time comes, it is entirely possible that two main spheres of economic activity will become gradually defined: the sphere of government-controlled, or government-guided, economy, embracing enterprises necessary for the public welfare, and not particularly inviting for the investment of private capital, such as public utilities and railways, which before World War II were already under government control in many European countries; and the sphere of private enterprise, notably the production of consumers' goods, where variety of wares is a special inducement to consumers. No rigid demarcation between the two spheres is either possible or desirable at a time when national and international economies are in a state of flux. But one thing we may expect; and that is that any form of private enterprise will be increasingly judged not in terms of its gainfulness, but in terms of the contribution it makes to the welfare of the community as a whole.

When we speak of government control over economic

174

activities, the impression is often given that the "government" is something apart or above the people—some kind of abstract, unseen, and somehow evil force which seeks to bedevil and oppress the individual. If democracy is a living thing, and not only a Fourth of July peroration, then the government is—or should be—ourselves, bone of our bone and flesh of our flesh. Then, when we say that this or that enterprise is "government-controlled," or "government-owned," or "government-regulated," what we mean is that we, the people of the country, control it, or own it, or regulate it—and do so not to bedevil or oppress anyone, but to enhance the common good. For if we, as a people, reach the conclusion that national wealth is better spent on hospitals, parks, schools, museums, and libraries—on better and still better medical, educational, and recreational services for all of us—than on luxuries for any one of us, we have the perfect right, by common consent, to spend our wealth that way rather than another. Of course we must never forget, as some reformers seem to do, that before we can spend anything at all we must first produce the national wealth. But this production does not mean merely the investment of money; what it means, first and foremost, is the use of labor, managerial ability, and scientific inventiveness. So the question boils down to this: Do we, and the peoples of the other United Nations, want after this war to devote our labor, managerial ability, and scientific inventiveness to the development of an economic system that will provide greater opportunities for human beings everywhere to attain a minimum standard of living, even though this may mean that some of us will gain far less financially than in the past, and all of us may have to put up with some discomforts and difficulties during the transition period after the war, before we can get reconstruction under way?

175

One answer to this question has already been given by the British with the publication of the Beveridge report.[1] This report, as Sir William Beveridge himself points out, is not a revolutionary program; nor does it attempt to provide a comprehensive social policy for Britain, or set down the conditions under which national wealth can be produced. It is concerned "with so distributing whatever wealth is available to them in total, as to deal first with first things, with essential physical needs." It reflects the belief that "the object of government in peace and in war is not the glory of rulers or of races, but the happiness of the common man."

This report, which unifies all existing forms of insurance in Britain, and makes special provisions for medical, maternity, and burial benefits—thus providing security to the individual from the cradle to the grave—expresses the view that security can be combined with freedom, and enterprise, and responsibility of the individual for his own life. The Beveridge plan does not give anyone something for nothing. In its own words, it merely assures "income for subsistence on condition of service and contribution and in order to make and keep men fit for service." Over and above the subsistence level it leaves "room and encouragement to all individuals to win for themselves something above the national minimum." As the British have discovered through bitter experience, individual initiative and incentive are far more quickly killed by the dole, which demoralizes and disheartens men and women, than by a minimum subsistence to which the state, the employer, and the worker will all be expected to contribute, and which will come to the beneficiary not as charity, but as the fruit of his own efforts.

[1] *Social Insturance and Allied Services* (New York: The Macmillan Co., 1942). See pp. 170-72.

The program set forth in the Beveridge report is full of valuable suggestions for any program of reconstruction the United Nations may undertake after the war. When Vice President Wallace spoke of "a quart of milk a day" for everyone, he used a symbol familiar to us—although not to many other peoples—for what Beveridge would call "subsistence." By assisting backward peoples to achieve a subsistence standard of living we shall not be robbing them of incentive or the will to improve their own existence through their own efforts. In many instances we may be helping them to find the incentive to live at all. Those who oppose participation by the United States in relief and rehabilitation measures after the war are as short-sighted in international affairs as some of the sweatshop employers of the worst days of the Industrial Revolution, who thought that ill-paid, ill-fed, ill-housed workers could produce satisfactory work, and would remain permanently contented with their lot. To use Beveridge's phrase, which he applied only to Britain, democracy must "free itself once for all of the scandal of physical want for which there is no economic or moral justification."

The trail blazed by the Beveridge report, and by our own drafts of social security legislation, should be open to all countries, and should become the well-traveled road of the future. Most human beings are concerned, first of all, not with the intricacies of diplomacy, nor with territorial boundaries, nor with the reshuffling of colonies, nor with access to raw materials, but with the humble yet all-essential needs of daily living—with food, and housing, and education, and health, and the bringing up of children. Dimly, but with ever-increasing emotion, on whatever military or civilian front they may be fighting, they are beginning to realize that they want not only to survive but to create a world in which it is worth while surviving.

177

The question whether by effecting improvements in human welfare we shall prevent wars cannot be answered as yet in the affirmative. Wars do not spring solely from economic conflicts and economic dislocations, but these conflicts and dislocations within nations do tempt people to indulge in political adventures to improve their conditions, and to follow leaders who promise them a "new order." By taking measures to improve human welfare we may not eliminate all causes of wars, but we may succeed in removing some of the difficulties that create national political ferment and provoke international clashes.

But, as Sir William Beveridge has rightly pointed out: "Freedom from want cannot be forced on a democracy or given to a democracy. It must be won by them. Winning it needs courage and faith and a sense of national unity: courage to face facts and difficulties and overcome them; faith in our future and in the ideals of fair-play and freedom for which century after century our forefathers were prepared to die; a sense of national unity overriding the interests of any class or section." Sir William was here speaking about Britain. But, paraphrasing his words, we might say that we cannot force freedom from want on other countries. China, and India, and the countries of Latin America and the Balkans will all have to take responsibility for the social welfare of their own people, just as we ourselves must take the responsibility for improving our own welfare here. But what we, and the British, and other nations that have gained experience with modern industrial techniques can do is to share this experience with others, on the assumption that a world half starved and half fed is not a world that will long be safe for political democracy. It is in the hands of all of us— the common men and women of whom Wallace and Beveridge are speaking—to become masters of our dreams.

THE HEALTH OF THE WORLD COMMUNITY

CHARLES-EDWARD A. WINSLOW
Professor of Public Health, Yale School of Medicine
New Haven, Connecticut

THE WORLD WAR IN WHICH WE ARE ENGAGED IS NOT—like many conflicts of the past—a war for the power or prestige of individual nations. It is a war for a way of life. The new order we are seeking differs from that of the Nazis precisely in the fact that it is based on a Christian ideal—the concept that every individual born into the world has a unique and special value. The word "democracy" means something more fundamental than the privilege of casting a vote. Julian Huxley, in an article in *Harper's Magazine* for September, 1942, said:

> Our first problem is then to find a criterion or a principle of democracy which is universal and is applicable in every period of history, under any conceivable set of conditions. So far as I can see, there is only one such criterion—the individual human being, his needs and his development. The yardstick by which we can measure democratic achievement is the satisfaction of the needs of human individuals. . . . . Every human being born into the world has in the eyes of true democracy a certain individual birthright—a birthright of health, strength, intelligence, varied enjoyment, and free interest, which must not be denied or stunted if the society into which he is born lays claim to being democratic.

In direct opposition to such a vision stands the ideology of Berlin and Tokyo. The mad masters of Germany and Japan deny "intelligence" and "varied enjoyment" and "free interest" even to the sodden masses of their own peoples. They have sought by systematic robbery and murder to crush out the "health" and "strength" of the subjugated nations of Europe and of Asia. They have brought some measure of suffering and sacrifice to all the peoples of the world, to Africa, to Oceania, to us in the remote Americas. We must build the new order of democracy not on the relatively solid and relatively comfortable foundation of 1939 but on a world in ruins.

The mystical symbolism of the sixth chapter of Revelation has a pregnant message for us today. The white horse of ruthless power, the red horse of war, the black horse of famine, and the pale horse of death are still stablemates; and their deadly riders exercise dominion, as John predicted, "over the fourth part of the earth." The results of such a world catastrophe can be only dimly visualized. If not controlled by an effective and enlightened world order, they may well repeat the human suffering and social dislocation which accompanied and followed the Black Death of the fourteenth century.

The advance of medical science has taught us that even in normal times, in a country so prosperous as the United States, a quarter or more of our children suffer from minor dietary deficiencies which, in subtle but demonstrable degree, handicap them in health and efficiency and satisfaction. Consider what the situation must be in Greece, in Jugoslavia, in Poland, in France—what it will be on the whole continent of Europe and in much of Asia tomorrow.

Disease follows famine as inevitably as famine follows war. Tuberculosis—our most sensitive index of health status—increased its death toll in Germany by 57 per cent in 1918 as compared with 1914. With the additive effects of mass migration, lack of medical service, and breakdown of community controls, more dramatic manifestations of herd infection are certain to appear. In the Soviet Union between 1917 and 1921 there were more than twenty-five million cases of typhus fever, with over two and a half million deaths.

When this epidemic of typhus was brought back to Poland by masses of returning expatriates, I had an opportunity of observing it at first hand and of realizing to the full the historic continuity which unites the twin phenomena of war and pestilence. There was a French member of our mission whose grandfather was a physician of the Grande Armée during Napoleon's retreat from Moscow. In Vilna, in Grodno, in Bialystok there were public meetings, and at every meeting Colonel Gauthier made a speech about his grandfather's experience with typhus in that town a century before. It did grow a bit monotonous after a time, but it was vitally significant to see the same tragic drama pursuing its same course in the same places and under the same circumstances after a hundred years. Last fall we heard sinister rumors that typhus was for a third time on the march in exactly the same Vilna-Grodno-Bialystok triangle.

With such problems as these we must deal when the guns cease firing. The challenge will not come all at once, but gradually, with the occupation of each particular area which our arms can free from the stifling grasp of the enemy. It has already come in North Africa, where we are now demonstrating the difference between the Axis concept of a dominated people as a source of plunder and the United Nations vision of brotherly co-operation in national rehabilitation. Governor Lehman is already setting up far-reaching machinery for bringing essential food supplies to the people of Morocco and Algeria.

It is unfortunate that even on such a clear issue as this there is not yet unanimity among the American people. Senator Nye of North Dakota has recently said: "It might be necessary to keep the American Army functioning and ready to hold down the Chinese and others, who don't like and won't drink milk, while Henry Wallace pours milk down their throats." This gentleman is not prepared to carry his acceptance of human brotherhood so far as to grant that the Chinese enjoy even a common bond of a stomach with his lordly self. Shakespeare has a different message on this point. He says, "Hath not a Jew eyes? hath not a Jew hands, organs, dimensions, senses, affections, passions? fed with the same food, hurt with the same weapons, subject to the same diseases, healed by the same means, warmed and cooled by the same winter and summer, as a Christian is?"

Even the Hottentot needs calories and salts and vitamins. He must have the same energy to carry on the activities of his daily life that we require. He needs the same forty or so essential materials—calcium, phosphorus, tyrosin, leucin, ascorbic acid, thiamin hydrochloride—that we must have to build up our body tissues and regulate our physiological processes.

We must do our share in feeding the hungry, with the other more fortunate nations of the earth, because we are Christians and recognize our moral responsibilities as members of the human race. We must also undertake the task because to do so is the only course of intelligent self-interest. The "American standard of living" in a world of radio and airways is no longer possible behind the ostrich walls of national isolation. It can and must depend on a democratic world order in which alone a democratic state can function, and no world order can be built on a foundation of half-starved peoples. The madness of Germany today has its strongest roots in the generation that was underfed a quarter of a century ago.

In the immediate postwar period, and thereafter, it will be our task to see that the people of liberated areas are not only fed but provided with necessary basic health protective services. President A. Lawrence Lowell of Harvard once said:

> It is hardly an exaggeration to summarize the history of four hundred years by saying that the leading idea of a conquering nation in relation to the conquered was in 1600 to change their religion; in 1700 to change their laws; in 1800 to change their trade; and in 1900 to change their drainage. May we not say that on the prow of the conquering ship in these four hundred years, first stood the priest, then the lawyer, then the merchant, and finally the physician.

As we move into occupied territories we shall be faced with urgent disease problems. It will be essential to purify polluted water supplies and construct new and better ones, to control insect carriers of disease, to establish emergency hospitals and quarantine stations, to distribute curative and preventive serums and vaccines. The problem, however, involves much more than temporary emergency service. It requires for true long-range effectiveness the development of lasting public-health machinery for the maintenance of adequate health standards in the years to come.

Here we have a very special contribution to make. One of the major social advances of the past quarter century in the United States has been a concrete definition of the communal machinery necessary for the attainment of a reasonable health ideal. Such machinery has, it is true, been fully developed only in certain fortunate areas of even our own country. In other parts of the world local factors make the problems more serious, and economic limitations render their solution more difficult. Yet we are fighting this war for the cause of democracy; and the inescapable challenge of democracy is the opportunity for every human being to develop his body, his mind, and his spirit to the maximum of individual possibility.

The ultimate ideals we must have in mind have been suggested in a definition of public health as

the science and the art of preventing disease, prolonging life, and promoting physical and mental health and efficiency through organized community efforts for the sanitation of the environment, the control of community infections, the education of the individual in principles of personal hygiene, the organization of medical and nursing service for the early diagnosis and preventive treatment of disease, and the development of social machinery which will ensure to every individual in the community a standard of living adequate for the maintenance of health.

The more specific objectives implied in this broad definition may be briefly summarized as follows:

I. *Sanitation of the Environment*

1. Provision of an adequate supply of drinking water of safe sanitary quality. This is an end which has been more or less fully attained in the more fortunate countries, but which remains challenging in those regions—such as India—where cholera and typhoid fever still prevail.

2. Protection of the sanitary quality of milk and other

foods which are likely to become contaminated with disease-producing microbes. The heavy toll taken by dysentery in many tropical and subtropical areas is an outstanding example of the importance of such procedures.

3. The sanitary disposal of wastes, particularly those which may be contaminated with human excreta.

4. The control of insects and other vermin which may serve as the carriers and spreaders of the germs of disease. The tremendous importance of this problem is indicated by the existence in the United States, as well as in every other continent, of extensive areas in which wild rodents harbor the germ of bubonic plague, and by the presence in Africa and South America of vast regions in which wild animals and insects constitute similar foci of yellow fever.

5. The control of hazards in industry due to poisons such as lead, solvents, and carbon monoxide, and to harmful dusts, particularly silica. The probable rapid industrialization of previously nonindustrial countries in the postwar period will greatly increase such hazards.

6. Protection against conditions which lead to mechanical accident and injury. Mechanization of industry and the development of motor transport have greatly multiplied these risks so that 100,000 deaths a year are credited to "accidental" causes in the United States alone.

II. *Control of Community Infections*

1. A well-equipped epidemiological service for the detection and isolation and quarantine of diseases spread largely by direct transfer from person to person. This service depends on the functioning of a good public-health laboratory.

2. Provision of an ample supply of specifically preventive and curative serums and vaccines and drugs. Diphtheria has been practically eliminated from many regions

185

by such provision, and the sulfa drugs now promise control of such age-old scourges as pneumonia and gonorrhea.

3. A specially organized community program for the control of tuberculosis, including public-health nursing and clinic service for case finding, clinics and sanatoriums for treatment, and follow-up for aftercare of arrested cases.

4. An intensive program for the detection and clinic treatmen⸱ of syphilis and gonorrhea and for the epidemiological and social control of factors which promote venereal infection.

5. In tropical areas, similar co-ordinated campaigns for the detection and treatment and control of hookworm disease and malaria. Hookworm infection is seriously prevalent in areas where 900,000,000 out of the 1,700,000,000 of the earth's inhabitants reside. Of malaria Osler once said: "If a census were taken among the world's workers on disease, the judgment to be based on the damage to health and direct mortality, the votes would be given to malaria as the greatest single destroyer of the human race."

III. *Education of the Individual in the Principles of Personal Hygiene*

1. The organization within any given area of a comprehensive educational program for familiarizing the people of that area with their major health problems, with the community facilities for dealing with those problems, and with the responsibility of the individual for the promotion of his own health.

2. The development of a public-health nursing staff to furnish that personal health guidance in the home which is essential in order to translate general principles into personal application. Standards in the United States call for one public-health nurse for every two thousand persons in the population. In many areas health educators of

a less fully trained type may be utilized, as has been done with success in certain communities in the Philippines.

3. The organization of a comprehensive program for the protection of the health of mothers and infants, including prenatal clinics, delivery service, *post partum* care, child health conferences, and nursing supervision. The program of the U.S.S.R. along these lines has been specially notable, as has that of New Zealand.

4. The development of a co-ordinated plan for promoting the health of school children, including sanitation of school buildings; promotion of sound mental hygiene in the classroom; education in the basic principles of healthful living, physical education, and recreational activity; and the periodic medical inspection of the school child.

IV. *Organization of Medical and Nursing Services for the Early Diagnosis and Preventive Treatment of Disease*

There is no sharp limit which can be drawn between preventive and curative medical care. An adequate health program for any country cannot be assured without taking its entire medical facilities into account. The ideals for such facilities may be summarized as follows, although they represent standards which will for long be unattainable except in relatively prosperous areas.

1. Hospital facilities. Our accepted standards in the United States call for 460 general hospital beds, 560 mental hospital beds, and 140 beds for tuberculosis per 100,000 persons in the population. We actually have now available 730 of the grand total of 1,160 proposed for all three types of beds. It is of interest to note that during the present crisis increasing use of hospital facilities in the United States has demonstrated that our ideal allotments for hospital facilities were by no means too high.

187

2. Physicians. In this respect the United States is more fortunate than any other large country, having 126 physicians for every 100,000 persons in the population. Careful study of ideal needs has shown that a slightly greater supply of physicians could be utilized to advantage.

3. Nurses. Here again the United States is unusually fortunate, with 179 nurses for every 100,000 persons. Here also it appears certain that even a slightly larger proportion of nurses would be ideally desirable.

4. Midwives. So far as the problem of childbirth is concerned, the experience of such countries as Holland and the very low maternal mortality recorded for such countries demonstrates the great value of the trained midwife. Similar success has been attained by the use of nurse-midwives in the Appalachian Mountain region of the United States. Holland has had about 12 midwives for each 100,000 persons in the population.

5. Dentists. An adequate supply of dentists has never been approached, even in the most favored countries. A reasonably sound program can be developed only by concentrating on the correction of dental defects of children before the more serious stages of dental decay have been reached.

6. Organization. Even when such general quantitative standards of personnel as have been reviewed above are met, they will scarcely prove adequate without effective organization secured through the association of doctors, nurses, dentists, and other personnel around hospitals in organized service groups. Such group practice is essential, not only for economy of time and effort, but also for ensuring a reasonable quality of service through mutual contact and supervision.

7. Payment for service. The best potential medical resources will not be effective unless they are actually made

available to the people who need service under financial conditions which can be met without sacrifice of other essentials of life and without loss of self-respect. This means that—except for the very highest economic levels —the costs of medical care must be placed on a group payment basis through the use of insurance or taxation or some combination of both methods. Voluntary group insurance may serve for the middle economic level; compulsory insurance seems the most generally useful procedure for industrial workers; tax-supported medical care will often be the solution for rural areas.

8. Mental hygiene. The development of a really comprehensive program for the promotion of mental and emotional health is an ideal which lies beyond the horizon of the future. Nearly one half of all hospital beds in the United States are, however, occupied by patients suffering from mental and nervous diseases; and the burden placed upon the average family through minor mental and emotional maladjustments is probably similarly equal to the burden caused by all other types of disease. It is therefore of vital importance that the beginnings which have—here and there—been made in the development of child-guidance clinics, mental-hygiene clinics, and the like should be greatly extended in the future.

V. A Standard of Living Adequate for the Maintenance of Health

So far we have been chiefly considering measures designed for the prevention of specific types of disease and for the treatment of such diseases. In the future we shall be more and more concerned with the promotion of health in a positive sense, and it is in this field that the social and economic world in which men live becomes of primary

189

importance. Progress along at least three major lines is essential to the realization of our ideals.

1. Nutrition. Beyond the immediate challenge of dealing with the starvation in war-torn areas lies the more far-reaching problem of continuing adequate nutrition for all nations. This involves comprehensive planning in regard to the production and distribution of essential foods —particularly those containing necessary salts and vitamins—so that the right kinds of nutriment can be obtained by the people at a price within their means. What can be accomplished by such a program is well illustrated by the experience of England, where under the stress of war local food production has been doubled and, by rationing at the top and government and industrial canteens at the bottom, the nutritional status of the total population has been vastly improved.

2. Housing. Nutritional needs are reasonably uniform throughout the world, aside from the greater energy needs in cold climates. Housing needs vary much more widely. In the tropics there is no problem of keeping warm in winter, in the far north no difficulty in keeping cool in summer. Water supply and waste disposal, while of primary importance in a Malayan village, are automatically cared for in a modern city. On the other hand, noise hazards, lack of play space, dangers from gas and electricity, provisions for escape in case of fire, are of major significance for the city tenement but present no problems in the jungle. Other housing problems vary in their immediate importance with general levels of social development. Artificial illumination is less significant in an illiterate population. Backward races are accustomed to overcrowding, to lack of privacy, to primitive cooking equipment. Such differences, however, should decrease in a

190

postwar world pledged to diminish the gross inequalities of opportunity now offered to the races of mankind. Furthermore, the inevitable industrialization of countries like China and India is likely to superpose some of the worst new problems of mechanized civilization upon the ancient handicaps associated with a simpler culture. Within the limits set by such local variables there are certain basic needs which must be met. They may be summarized as follows:

a) Basic physiological needs. Here must be included, in the necessary objectives of a healthful dwelling: protection against excessive heat and cold, provision of adequate natural illumination at night, protection against excessive noise, provision of adequate space for exercise and for the play of children.

b) Basic psychological needs. Equally important from the standpoint of mental and emotional health are the following essentials: adequate privacy for the individual, opportunity for normal family and community life, facilities for the performance of household tasks with a minimum of fatigue (60 hours of housework per week are performed in the average American home), facilities for cleanliness of the person and the dwelling, and provision of possibilities for aesthetic satisfaction and concordance with prevailing local social standards (the sense of inferiority associated with a home notably below the standards of friends and neighbors may produce emotional reactions having the most serious influence upon mental health).

c) Sanitation. Essential factors in good housing are the provision of a safe water supply; adequate methods of disposal of excretal wastes; protection against rats, flies, and other vermin which may transmit disease; provision of facilities for the storage and preservation of food; and

191

avoidance of room overcrowding which favors contact infection.

d) Safety. Here we must provide against the hazards of structural collapse, of fire, of electrical shocks and burns, and of falls and other mechanical injuries. Some 30,000 fatal accidents occur each year in American homes.

Any sound program of housing must be concerned, not only with the individual house as a separate dwelling unit, but with the much broader aspects of community planning. The modern housing movement aims at more than healthful homes; it seeks to create healthful neighborhoods. The isolated tenement dweller, without social roots and social responsibilities, is the ideal material for the dictator and his loud-speaker. The roots of international solidarity and national solidarity must be founded on the evolution of the mutual responsibilities of a neighborhood.

The probable extension of methods of prefabrication will greatly increase the need for community planning in the postwar period. The purchase of low-cost prefabricated houses and their haphazard erection on any site controlled for the moment by their purchaser could create worse slums than those of the past. A house must be integrated into a network of water pipes and sewers and utility lines of various sorts. A home must be integrated into a similar complex of social relationships, industrial, commercial, educational, and recreational.

Furthermore, the local and regional planning of the future is intimately bound up with broad policies of land utilization. Large-scale development of land use in the broad public interest is absolutely essential, for it is speculative development of individual parcels which has created the slums of our chaotic industrial cities. The Final Report of the Expert Committee on Compensation and Betterment of the Ministry of Works and Planning of Great Britain is an excellent example of a basic attack on this problem, and the National Association of Housing Officials is preparing a constructive memorandum on postwar housing for the United States.

3. Social security. In industrial societies a third problem, that of social security, enters as an essential factor into the national health program. The complex machinery of industrialization has created new hazards of unemployment unknown in more primitive communities, and has materially weakened the unity of the family, which in simpler days to some extent absorbed the shock of sickness and old age. To provide a minimum degree of protection for the physical, and still more for the emotional, health of the population, a program of social insurance is essential to cover the three major hazards of:

a) Sickness.
b) Old age.
c) Unemployment.

The recent report by Sir William Beveridge on *Social Insurance and Allied Services* in Great Britain is an excellent example of a broad approach to this important problem.

To move toward such health goals as have been outlined above—ultimately to be visualized as essential for all the diverse cultures of this globe of ours—will require intensive study and continuous planning. It must have the leadership of the best thought of experts in all countries. How successful such leadership may be was demonstrated by the League of Nations after the last war. A special Epidemic Commission was created to deal with the 1921 typhus epidemic in Poland, to which I have referred above, and two years later was merged in the Health Section of the League. After dealing with the 1921 typhus epidemic the League was called upon to cope with grave sanitary problems created by the million or more destitute refugees

193

who poured into Greece as a result of the Turkish War. These refugees were promptly protected by vaccination against smallpox, cholera, and typhoid; and what threatened to be a serious epidemic catastrophe was reduced to a minor one. Sleeping sickness in equatorial Africa and malaria in Russia and the Balkans were studied by special commissions appointed for that purpose.

The role played by the League in connection with malaria in Greece has special historical significance. The disease was introduced into the Attic peninsula in the fourth century B.C., just at the time of the maximum glory of Athens. Many authorities believe that the decline of the great Grecian civilization was due to this cause, and the explanation is perhaps the most plausible one which has been offered to explain that phenomenon. Be that as it may, Greece was certainly crippled by malaria for some two thousand years. Finally the government appealed to the Health Committee of the League for aid. Expert advisers, armed with the best knowledge of all nations, were sent to Athens and conducted a control campaign which accomplished notable results. The gallant stand of Greece in 1941—which perhaps saved the whole Mediterranean for civilization—may well have been made possible by this achievement.

Less spectacular but no less important were the contributions of the Health Committee to the day-by-day routine of mobilization for defense against disease. At Geneva there was set up an epidemiological intelligence service to collect and disseminate by bulletins, and by telegraph or radio when necessary, information with regard to the prevalence of epidemic diseases of all sorts throughout the world. A branch office was established at Singapore in the heart of the epidemic danger zone, and to the horror of conservative officials warnings of infection in seaports were broadcast in clear so that the captain of any vessel might pick them up and guide his course accordingly. Biological products such as antitoxins and essential drugs were standardized for potency by international commissions so that doctors in all countries could rely upon a standard terminology and a standard dosage. Results of the treatment of cancer in various countries were compared and interpreted, and uniform methods of analysis agreed upon.

Even more significant, perhaps, than some of these direct services was the indirect result of the program for interchange of sanitary personnel. Thanks to the generous support of the Rockefeller Foundation, the Health Section arranged each year for study tours in which the best health practices of one or more nations were observed by groups of leading health officials from other countries. The personal contact thus fostered among the officials of Europe and the United States and Latin America was of incalculable value in promoting a co-operative spirit and in disseminating knowledge of sound administrative practice.

The Health Section of the League did not, however, limit itself to the more traditional problems of sanitation and epidemic disease control. Its leaders saw clearly that the public health of the future must concern itself with the promotion of health in a positive sense. It must be considered not only as an engineering science, not only as a medical science, but also as a social science. Clearly visualizing this ideal, the League made important fundamental studies of social security, particularly of health insurance, of nutrition, and of housing.

The Health Section was first drawn into the field of dietary hygiene by a request for aid from the government of Chile. It established international committees, including the ablest leaders of the United States and Great

195

Britain, and stimulated the formation of national nutrition committees in twenty countries. The standards established at Geneva as to the quantities of various nutrients necessary to maintain health are basic in sound practice throughout the world. Our own Committee on the Hygiene of Housing in the United States was established at the request of the Health Section of the League to serve as its corresponding agency in the United States.

The staff of the Health Section at Geneva is now reduced to two persons. The marble halls overlooking Lake Leman echo only to the occasional footsteps of caretakers. Yet the waves of influence set in motion there continue to influence and to activate social progress in many countries of the world. After the war we may well turn again to the rudiments of machinery for international co-operation which remain in being at Geneva. If that is not expedient, we shall be forced to create under some new name a new organization on essentially the same pattern as that of the Health Section of the League.

The world health organization of the future must, however, have one major function which was not highly developed in the program of its predecessor—a function which has been performed in the past by another major agency in the health field, The International Health Division of the Rockefeller Foundation.

The late Hermann M. Biggs based his notable contributions to the cause of public health in the United States on the principle that "public health is purchasable. Within natural limitations a community can determine its own death rate." This principle has a necessary corollary, that "without money you cannot purchase public health." The type of public-health organization which we visualize as adequate in the United States requires for a community of 100,000 persons—in the field of public health alone,

196

exclusive of the treatment of the sick—the time of some 8 physicians, 46 nurses, and about 30 other persons, including sanitary inspectors, laboratory experts, statisticians, and clerks. Such a program will cost about two dollars per year per person in the population served. Even in the United States there are many counties and some entire states which actually lack the funds to pay such an amount for public health from their own resources without taxes heavier than their populations can bear. For this reason we have developed a program of grants-in-aid from the national government for the development of essential public-health services throughout the country, on the sound assumption that disease recognizes no political boundaries and that no nation can be healthy unless all its parts have attained at least a minimum of health security.

What is true of a vast, diversified nation is true of the whole world. Therefore an essential function of the international health organization of the future must be the provision of judiciously guarded grants-in-aid to nations whoses own resources do not permit them to develop their own health standards to the level which international security demands. The experience of the Rockefeller Foundation shows how fruitful such a policy may be, and our present lend-lease agreements with the United Nations open the door to such a policy on a wider scale. The grants should not come directly from one country alone, but should be administered through a comity of nations. They should be grants and not loans in the technical sense; but they will be in effect loans, since they will build up in the less advanced nations and areas prosperity and purchasing power which will ultimately redound to the benefit of all.

It should, however, be emphasized that such a program, either on a national or an international basis, is in the nature of a temporary stopgap. The word "temporary" may indeed be interpreted in terms of decades; but subsidy as between one area and another, one nation and another, as a permanent arrangement cannot be consonant with self-respect. Our ideal must be ultimate economic as well as political independence. Where a given nation is now on an economic level too low for the provision of the basic decencies of life, the most important service we can render to that nation is to make an intensive study of its resources in manpower and materials and try to devise a program of national self-support on a level consonant with democratic opportunity. Sometimes the best contribution we can make to the health of an area would be to build a railroad or to remove inhibiting economic barriers to trade.

The possibility of creating a new world order based on such principles of co-operation depends first and foremost on the attitude of the United States of America. In 1920 we threw away the peace after having won the war by retiring into our shell of isolationism and refusing to share any responsibility for the future of the world. Some lessons I think we have learned in the twenty years that have gone. It seems probable that the American people are now willing to assume their share in the maintenance of order. But mere policing is not enough. The Atlantic Charter visualizes "freedom from want" as well as "freedom from fear." Indeed, freedom from the fear of war cannot be really assured unless freedom from want is also attained. Peace based on armed force alone and not on the consent of reasonably contented peoples can never be permanent and secure. This is why the Commission to Study the Organization of Peace has declared:

The Commission aims to do its utmost to lead the American people to see more clearly than they did twenty years ago

198

that, for selfish and unselfish reasons alike, all their efforts must have as their ultimate goal the creation of a better world in which to live—a world in which international cooperation will be able to use human intelligence and natural resources for the economic security and free development of all men..... Peace under modern conditions cannot be a static condition of life achieved by the renunciation of war, nor a mere pious desire to live at peace. Peace must be a dynamic and continuous process for the achievement of freedom, justice, progress, and security on a world-wide scale.

Such an ideal is not unattainable. Donald M. Nelson tells us:

For a generation we have been living on the edge of a new world; we are only beginning to realize it. For the first time in the history of the human race there can be enough of everything to go around. Poverty is not inevitable any more. The sum total of the world's greatest output of goods divided by the sum total of the world's inhabitants no longer means a little less than enough for everybody. It means more than enough. The possibilities in that simple statement are beyond calculation—and what we are fighting for is the right to turn some of those possibilities into realities.

To win *this* fight, the United States must be ready to sacrifice not only the blood of its young men in the primary conflict but some of its special economic privileges in the days after the guns have ceased firing. Access to essential raw materials, freedom from excessive tariffs and all unreasonable barriers to trade, must be basic in the postwar world if that world is to endure.

To attain the acceptance by the United States of such a program will not be easy. The McCormicks and the Pattersons, all the sinister isolationist forces which opposed preparation for the war, now oppose preparation for the peace. It is said on credible authority that some thirty members of the United States Senate are already banded together to wreck any serious attempt at international co-operative effort. They staged in December a fight against a minor agreement with the Republic of Panama which was essentially a dress rehearsal of the battle they intend to wage against the participation of our country in a sane world order.

It is possible to demonstrate beyond peradventure the practical folly of isolationism. It is clear as crystal that the sacrifice of blood and treasure we are making in 1943 will be completely wasted if we do not co-operate—both politically and economically—in the upbuilding of global peace. Yet it may be that the most powerful argument which we can present to the American people against the policy of "this little band of willful men" is not that of self-interest. It is after all the human will, the human sense of moral and spiritual values, which determines human conduct. Perhaps the ultimate challenge in the campaign which must be fought on the floors of Congress and in the polling booths of every city and village of our land will be that ancient and inexorable challenge, "Am I my brother's keeper?"

CHRISTIANITY AND THE WORKERS OF THE WORLD

CARTER GOODRICH

Professor of Economics, Columbia University, and Chairman of the Governing Body of the International Labor Office

IN CONSIDERING THE POSITION OF THE WORKERS IN THE POST-war world, I should like to discuss the promises that have been made to them and the demands that they will make, and to ask what we ought to do in dealing with these demands and fulfilling these promises.

Let us begin with the promises that have been held out to the workers and to the common peoples of the world on behalf of the United Nations. The fifth point of the Atlantic Charter proclaims the objectives of "improved labor standards, economic advancement and social security." Article VII of the Lend-Lease Agreement pledges measures "directed to the expansion .... of production, employment, and the exchange and consumption of goods which are the material foundations of the liberty and welfare of all peoples." These official pronouncements of policy have been restated and put into warmer and more human terms by the leaders of the United Nations. Notable among such declarations are the President's unforgettable statement on "The Four Freedoms"; the Vice President's speech on "The Century of the Common Man," which put these principles into the everyday terms of the breakfast table; Ambassador Winant's speech to the Durham miners urging a postwar "drive for houses" to replace the wartime "drive for tanks"; the emphasis on "full employment at good wages" in the recent Toronto address of the Under Secretary of State; and now the "full employment and full production for the benefit of the common man" of the memorable address with which this Conference was opened.

There are many others in this and other countries, and they have been paralleled by a series of equally noteworthy declarations made by responsible agencies of the Christian churches. The section on "The Church and Economic Reconstruction" contained in the most recent report of the Committee on the State of the Church of the Federal Council of Churches lists a number of these pronouncements and is itself a significant contribution to the discussion.

It is no new thing that statesmen should make sweeping promises to their peoples, particularly in time of war. They did it in the last war, and they have done it in this. It *is* a new thing that their emphasis should fall so largely on labor conditions and social welfare. Never has so much been promised in the social field. Never has there been such full realization that the fulfillment of these social promises rests on the creation of a sounder economic order. Never has there been such full realization that the ends of economic activity, as the President told the 1941 Conference of the International Labor Organization, *are* the social objectives.

I have referred to these promises, as you have seen, rather exultantly. But that is not the only way they have been received. Some Americans have dealt with them derisively. I will not give illustrations, and I do not think we need to take time to discuss them. Other doubts have been expressed, however, which we cannot dismiss so lightly. Certain questions have been raised by men of seriousness and good will. Should we, they ask, hold out such glowing hopes? Are we not promising more than we can possibly fulfill? Will not these declarations, therefore, lead merely to anger and disappointment and unrest? We know the perils of disillusionment. The challenge is a real one. It asks us to choose between two alternative policies: Shall we promise less and thus avoid disappointment, or shall we see see to it that we make good on the great promises?

I think I know which of these you will choose. I am sure I know which of them I should wish you to choose. But I should not be honest in asking you to take the bolder of the alternatives if I did not at the same time point out the reality of the obstacles that stand in the way. We think, I suppose, of the promises as coming due at the close of the war. There will, however, be much in the world situation after victory to make their fulfillment particularly difficult. As Secretary Hull has pointed out, "The people of many countries will be starving and without means of procuring food, homeless and without means of building shelter, their fields scorched, their cattle slaughtered, their tools gone, their factories and mines destroyed, their roads and transport wrecked." In these regions economic activity will be at a standstill because of physical devastation, lack of supplies, and perhaps the complete breakdown of political and so- cial and economic organization. In larger parts of the world, economic activity will have been proceeding at a furious pace, but largely in the production of goods that will no longer be needed in time of peace. The former situation will present the problem of primary poverty for sheer lack of food and clothing and machines and the very fabric of economic arrangements. The latter will present the danger of mass unemployment because of the dislo- cations involved in shifting from one type of industry to another, and the danger that the demand for peacetime commodities will not equal that for the goods of war. In certain areas, therefore, labor standards will necessarily be extremely low. Other areas will, in all probability, be

203

confronting the circumstances under which labor standards are typically broken down rather than raised.

It is at this moment and under these conditions that the promises come due for fulfillment. It is at this time, moreover, that the demands of the workers will be pressed with particular vigor. Those of you who remember the discussions of war aims that took place during the last war will have noticed that the voice of labor, or at least of international labor, has this time been less conspicuous in the discussions. For this there are a number of reasons. One is the suppression of the labor movement in Continental Europe, first in the Axis countries, and then in the occupied nations, so that what was during the last war an important and very vocal part of the international labor movement now is broken or driven underground or speaking with the voice of a few leaders in exile. Yet against this must be set the assured position of trade unionism in Great Britain and the greatly increased strength of labor in the United States.

The other reasons are of a quite different character. "This is labor's war" in a quite different sense from that of 1914-18, and it is recognized as such by the labor movement in each of the United Nations. The labor movement has long been the foe of Fascism, and in many cases it was readier than most other groups to recognize the necessity of fighting. It has no sympathy with the enemy powers. At least since the German invasion of Russia, there has not been within it even a substantial minority that was confused on the major issue. There has been in labor ranks no such pacifism as last time divided the British labor movement, and there have been so far no industrial disputes either in the United States or in any of the Allied countries comparable in seriousness to those which shook South Wales and the Clyde during the last war. This we should bear in mind so as to consider our own current controversies in their proper proportion.

Moreover, the labor movement has this time had much more to do with the direction of the war effort. On the political side the British Labour Party was given strong representation in the War Cabinet at the time of Dunkirk, and New Zealand and Australia have Labour governments. On the industrial side there have been notable attempts to draw the trade unions into direct responsibility in the organization of manpower. These have had very great success in Great Britain and considerable success elsewhere. They are beginning to show real vitality in certain parts of the United States program. Under these circumstances the leaders of labor in the Allied countries have been too heavily occupied in the war effort to be giving their major attention to postwar questions, and too loyal to the announced purposes of the United Nations to be raising strong notes of dissidence and distrust.

It would, however, be a great mistake to conclude from this that labor's demands will not be strongly pressed in the peace. Even the now submerged labor movement of Continental Europe will be heard. It is now playing a large part in the work of the underground. It should play a still larger part in the liberation of Europe, and the policy of our government should be such as to encourage it to this end. More generally, the spokesmen of labor will be in a stronger rather than a weaker position at the peace table for the very reason that they will speak more on the basis of responsible participation and less on the basis of dissidence and criticism than in the last war. Their position, moreover, will obviously be strengthened rather than weakened by the promises that have been made to them. Surely they will not ask for less this time because they have been promised more.

205

What, then, will be the demands of labor? There are at least three that will be common to the workers in many or in all countries: first, freedom of association; second, social security; third, full employment.

As early as October, 1941, the president of the American Federation of Labor declared that the right of the workers to belong to free democratic trade unions "must now be written into a world peace treaty and guaranteed by those who subscribe their names to the peace treaty." This is a demand that must be taken seriously. We have seen the menace to the world when freedom of association has been denied. It is now clear that the destruction of the labor movement was one of the things which made it easy for the leaders of the Axis to take their peoples on the path of war. We have no right to risk a repetition of that process. Moreover, we need the participation of the unions as well as of other occupational associations in the work of reconstruction. The International Labor Conference of 1941, which on the eve of Pearl Harbor brought together in this country the representatives of more than thirty freedom-loving nations, gave particular attention to the problem of "effective collaboration between the public authorities and workers' organizations and employers' organizations." It declared that real co-operation was possible "only within the framework of democratic political institutions which guaranteed the freedom of association of workers and employers"; and it underlined the special importance of such co-operation "after victory for the transition from war economy to peace economy and for the economic and social reconstruction of the world . . . . which will call for a gigantic and co-ordinated effort on the part of the public authorities, workers, and employers." A year later a distinguished group of Catholic leaders from a number of American nations, meeting as the Inter-American Seminar on Social Studies, arrived at similar conclusions. Starting from the assumption that "it is necessary to make economic life serve the general good of all mankind," the seminar declared that "the form of organization should be one that emphasized the free organizations of business, of labor, and of farmers and of the professions, assisted and supervised by government."

Obviously the precise formulation of a guarantee of freedom of association and of a guarantee acceptable to all of the United Nations offers great difficulties. There is no one pattern of organization applicable to all parts of the world. In many regions agricultural co-operatives or other associations of small farmers or peasants will be the dominant form. But whatever the form and whatever the difficulties, the development and strengthening throughout the world of associations representing the common man is an essential part of a world program. It is not only a demand of the workers; it is a prerequisite to the practical fulfillment of the promises of the statesmen.

The second demand is for social security. I do not need to emphasize its importance or its widespread appeal. Of these the best evidence is the world's reception to the publication of the Beveridge report [1]—on the one hand acclaim and deep popular interest throughout the United Nations, and on the other angry denunciation by the radios of Berlin and Rome. The basis for the two reactions was the same. On both sides of the battle lines the proposals were recognized as one important step toward converting the Atlantic Charter from words into deeds.

How fully and how rapidly the Beveridge proposals will

[1] See Sir William Beveridge, *Social Insurance and Allied Services* (New York: The Macmillan Co., 1942).

be put into effect is a question of active current controversy in Great Britain. Now, with the submission to Congress of the National Resources Planning Board's report on "Security, Work and Relief Policies," the same issue has become a matter of current controversy in our own country. Let me apply the same comment to these two sets of proposals: Their precise details may or may not stand, but the general direction of movement which they represent is an irresistible one. For the United States may I add that I believe that this applies both to the more adequate coverage of the risks with which our present system of social security deals and also to its extension to the great risk of disability.

The movement toward more adequate social security is irresistible because it conforms to an increasingly definite moral concensus throughout the free countries. This is, I believe, a clear lesson from the course of recent social history. One of the most significant facts in that history has been the development in so many parts of the world of measures for dealing with the common risks for which low-income groups cannot themselves adequately provide—unemployment, industrial accident and disease, invalidity, old age, and the rest. This development has included preventive action—in public health and industrial hygiene, in training and rehabilitation—as well as action for the maintenance of income. The measures adopted have differed widely from country to country. Progress has been stimulated by international emulation. In this process a notable part has been played by the series of conventions and recommendations adopted at conferences of the International Labor Office and by the expert advice given by its officials to many governments, including our own, in the setting up of their systems of social security.

"No country has yet succeeded in covering all the common risks or in organizing the fight against all the causes

208

of social insecurity." [2]   The Beveridge plan represents a bold attempt to do this for the special circumstances of Great Britain.   The Planning Board proposes what is perhaps an equally bold advance from the present position in the United States.   I hold no brief for the details of either.   Two things, however, are clear.   There is no demand on which the workers of the world are more certain to be united than for the comprehensive protection of social security, and courageous measures for meeting that demand are essential to the fulfillment of the pledges of the United Nations.

But social security alone, however important, is not enough.   No one has stated this more vigorously than Sir William Beveridge himself.   "Income security," he says, "which is all that can be given by social insurance, is so inadequate a provision for human happiness" that it should not be put forward "by itself as a sole or principal measure of reconstruction."   It must be accompanied by "the abolition of mass unemployment." [3]   The demand for full employment, the determination that mass unemployment shall not be allowed again, is the most basic social aim emerging from the war in the industrial countries.   As an American employer has said, "No nation which ignores this demand will have much of a chance in the postwar world."

To meet this demand, and to meet it in the difficult period of postwar transition, is the highest challenge to economic statesmanship.   Parts of the program are clear.   In the first place, the extensive machinery of placement and training now developed for the shift to war employment must not be scrapped when the war is over.   It must be adapted to the no less difficult task of transfer to the needs of peace.   There will be no less need than now for a trained

[2] Oswald Stein, "Building Social Security," *International Labour Review,* XLIV, 3 (September, 1941), p. 263.

[3] *Op. cit.,* pp. 163, 164.

employment service. There will be even more need for the readaptation of skills and for measures re-equipping the wounded and injured for useful activity.

In the second place, extensive programs of public works will have to be put into operation to take up part of the slack when the enormous demand for munitions is checked. Such measures, together with similar programs by private employers, require planning now, and to an encouraging degree are receiving such planning. Their application after the war will require skillful timing, since the object, as the Planning Board recognizes, is to "head off both boom and depression."

In the third place, it is essential to ensure a substantial demand for goods on the part of private consumers. The sale of defense bonds, the tax rebates, and the effects of the existing system of social security already do much toward this end. Perhaps more will have to be done by forms of compulsory saving not yet applied, or by arrangements for dismissal compensation such as those to which the Planning Board refers.

These parts of a program of full employment are fairly obvious. How much more the government will have to do either in regulating or in supplementing the demand for labor is not yet clear. We do know that it cannot permit failure. What is essential, to quote Beveridge again, is "an announced determination to use the powers of the State to whatever extent may prove necessary to ensure for all, not indeed absolute continuity of work, but a reasonable chance of productive employment."[4]

I have spoken of this as a national problem, but its solution requires international action as well. Certainly that is true if we add to full employment the other half of the

---

[4] *Ibid.*

phrase with which it has appeared again and again in I.L.O. discussions, "full employment and a rising standard of living." Certainly that is true if we are really to make full use for human needs of the world's productive resources whose potentialities we have so far succeeded in approaching only for the purposes of war. For some areas this is all too obvious. In the devastated regions the very means of employment—tools, livestock, and machines—will at the beginning have to be provided by international aid. I trust we shall not fail in our part of the task. In many other parts of the world—in China, for example, and in large parts of Latin America—progress toward employment at a reasonable standard of living will depend on an advance toward industrialization to be made possible by the export of capital from the more developed countries. I trust that we shall take our part in that also, and that we shall devise better safeguards both for the lending and for the borrowing nations than have existed in the past.

But this is not all. The workers in this country, as in every other country, stand to gain by a reopening of the outlets of international trade. We cannot hope for growing markets in an impoverished world. Whatever transitional difficulties may have to be faced in certain cases, American industry and American labor will have greater prospects and greater opportunities in a world of expanded trade and of international economic co-operation. This has been clear in the minds of those who drew up the declarations of the United Nations. The Lend-Lease Agreement pledges its signatories to "appropriate domestic and international measures" for the expansion of world production. The fifth point of the Atlantic Charter pledges "the fullest collaboration between all nations" as the means for securing "improved labor standards, economic advancement and social security." It is important also that it be clear in the minds of the leaders of labor. If it is not, there is danger that those in every land who would gain the most by the fullest use of the world's productive resources will on nationalistic and protectionist grounds be led to support the measures that will in fact defeat these aims.

The full realization of labor's demands and the full realization of the statesmen's promises require international action for the expansion of production and trade. They also require the international setting of labor standards. The principal agency in this field is the International Labor Organization. During the twenty years between the wars, a major part of its work was the development of a code of international minimum standards covering a wide range of labor and social questions. These were embodied in a series of conventions—labor treaties intended for acceptance as binding obligations—and of less formal recommendations, model codes, and resolutions. Two parts of the process deserve emphasis. The first is the active part taken by labor and industry. In every representative organ of the I.L.O. the spokesmen of the trade unions and of the employers' associations stand on the same footing as the representatives of government. To the annual International Labor Conferences, in whose prolonged and vigorous discussions the actual texts of these conventions are hammered out, each nation is entitled to send two government delegates, one workers' delegate, and one employers' delegate. The conclusions arrived at therefore reflect—in addition to all the crossplay of national differences—the driving power of labor for better conditions and the effort of employers to avoid the imposition of unworkable provisions. The second part of the process is the winning of national consent, since the standards adopted by the conference receive binding force within a nation only when ratified by its own national authorities.

Both these stages are slow and painstaking. In all, sixty-seven conventions have been adopted. Some have received wide acceptance; others have been little applied. The recent acceptance by Great Britain in mid wartime of the obligations of two conventions covering the treatment of colonial labor brings the total number of national acts of ratification to 886. In subject matter as well as in coverage the achievement has been uneven and incomplete· No way has been found of setting international standards of the amount of wages. On the other hand, agreements affecting hours of labor have had widespread influence. The field of social insurance has been particularly well covered. A comprehensive system of conventions, five of them ratified by our own Senate, extends protection to the seamen of the world. Other fields in which international action was particularly appropriate and has been particularly useful include the setting of standards for the treatment of native labor and the protection of migrants working in countries other than their own. Still other conventions deal with employment, with protection against industrial diseases and accident, with the prohibition of child labor, and with the protection of women and young persons. "Gradually but surely international standards of labor and social policy were being built up, and international obligations to maintain these standards were being increasingly accepted." [5]

This work of building an international labor code must be taken up again with greater vigor when the war is over. If we maintain our determination to create a world in the pattern of the Atlantic Charter and the master Lend-Lease Agreement, far greater progress in setting labor standards will be possible than in the past. It is important also that the work should be closely related to other parts of a gen-

[5] International Labour Office, *International Labour Code, 1939* (Montreal, 1941), p. xiii.

213

eral program of reconstruction. One consequence of the United Nations' victory will surely be the development of a new attitude and a new policy toward what have been the dependent peoples of the world. There is increasing recognition that such a program must include more vigorous action toward the raising of living standards. One condition of the exercise of trusteeship over any dependent people might well be the acceptance of the obligations of the existing I.L.O. conventions governing the treatment of native labor. Still more important than this initial step would be the creation in these areas of representative organs for the progressive advancement of labor and social standards.

Again, the setting of labor standards should, I believe, be an integral part of the policy of loans for reconstruction and development. The purpose of such loans, which are an essential element in any broad international program of reconstruction, is the advancement of the welfare of the masses of the people. To make sure that they do in fact serve this purpose and to give assurance in the lending countries that they will not merely give power over modern machinery to exploiters of ill-paid labor, such loans might well be granted only on the condition of the observance of certain minimum labor standards. At the beginning any such standards would have to be set modestly and realistically. The work simply would not go forward if wages on the Yangtze or the Amazon or even the Danube were to be the same as those upon the Ohio or the Tennessee. Yet here also a useful start could be made and machinery set up for the progressive advancement of standards with the aid of the International Labor Organization and by democratic methods similar to those which the I.L.O. has employed in preparing its code of international standards.

214

These are not the only uses that should be made of the International Labor Organization as an agency for meeting the demands of the workers and fulfilling the promises of the statesmen. From its foundation the I.L.O. has exerted an influence on opinion and policy on a considerably wider range of issues than those of specific labor regulations. Discussions in the annual Conferences have dealt with public policy in a broad rather than a restricted sense and have served to crystallize international opinion on social and economic issues. A particularly notable example of this leadership was given by the International Labor Conference of 1941. Bringing together the representatives of thirty-four member nations and meeting before the United States or any of the other American republics had entered the war, it provided a most important representative forum for the formulation and proclamation of the social aims of the freedom-loving nations. It was unequivocal on the issue of the war. Its discussions stressed the linkage of social and economic issues. They pointed clearly to the value of the I.L.O. as an agency for bringing into increasingly responsible partnership in international organization the great associations of labor and industry—associations whose opposition might wreck the whole world conception on which the Atlantic Charter is built, and whose active co-operation must be secured if the objectives of the Charter are to be fully achieved.

With these things in view, the government, employer, and worker delegates of the United States introduced into the Conference a resolution instructing the I.L.O. to study and prepare measures of reconstruction. This resolution, which was adopted unanimously and with enthusiasm, asserted "the desirability of associating the International Labor Organization with the planning and application of measures of reconstruction." It declared that the I.L.O., because it possessed "the confidence of the free peoples" and included "in its structure the representatives of workers and employers," was qualified to take part in this work in such a way "as to minimize misunderstanding and unrest and to promote a stable and enduring peace." In a similar spirit Mr. Eden, speaking in December, 1942, as the leader of the House of Commons, expressed the hope that the International Labor Organization would become "the main instrument giving effect to Article V of the Atlantic Charter."

The preamble to the constitution of the I.L.O. as adopted at the Paris Peace Conference contains the following clause: "Conditions of labor exist involving such injustice, hardship, and privations to large numbers of people as to produce unrest so great that the peace and harmony of the world are imperilled; and an improvement of those conditions is urgently required." All this remains true. Yet those who face the problem today do so with a better understanding of the linkage of social and economic policy. Their emphasis is less on the removal of specific abuses and more on a broad advance in the levels of production and consumption. "Freedom from want" is a bolder statement of purpose than the clause I have just read. Mr. Wallace's formulation, "to put God's earth more completely at the service of all mankind," is far more eloquent. Neither the leaders of the United Nations nor those who attempt to formulate the policy of the Christian church for the postwar world can remain content with even the best of what was attempted at Paris. Yet they will do well to keep in the forefront of their planning and their policy the profound truth written into the first clause of the I.L.O. constitution, that "universal peace . . . . can be established only if it is based upon social justice."

HUMAN CHARACTER AND WORLD ORDER

REINHOLD SCHAIRER

Visiting Professor of Education, New York University

VICE PRESIDENT WALLACE, IN THE OPENING LECTURE OF this series—an address which will be long remembered and read throughout Europe—reminded us that Christianity and religion should be more and more a practical formula and concept of life. This was the conviction of three great educators of the past, who led their nations from postwar chaos and misery on the slow way of education to a new firm foundation, so firm that even Nazism could not break it. These men were Grundtvig in Denmark and Pestalozzi and Fellenberg in Switzerland. Denmark and Switzerland learned in the last century the lesson which other nations still have to learn. They are the great models of educational reconstruction. All three educators knew that Jesus was a carpenter, Peter a fisherman, Paul a carpet weaver. Christianity intended to be, and will be in the future, either nothing at all or something as reliable, practicable, and real as a roof built by a good carpenter, a boat which a fisherman steers through the storm, or a carpet woven to keep tight and fine for centuries. Religion, said the great Czech educator Comenius, "is not the picture of a growing tree, but the tree itself."

Within the next five years we will know whether religion will survive as a great dynamic power or become weak and an outcast in the catacombs of earth. It can survive only if it helps to build the better new world order which must come into being during the stormy years after this war. Those five years ahead are the most decisive years of ours and the coming generations.

We now seem to be approaching a *military* victory, provided the United Nations unite more and more. But the *peace* victory is still uncertain. Will the forces of freedom, of Christian democracy, win—or will the world call for some other more effective formula? Those who hope and wish that our way of Christian democracy will lead us toward the future need to remember that this way has to be built and prepared as a new way. It is like approaching a new continent, still undiscovered; pioneering is again essential. All the forces which can be used in this construction, most of them pioneering forces, must be ready and intensively active and effective now.

If we here and now immediately make the decision to apply true Christianity—that is, the rule of brotherhood throughout the world, in deeds, not in words only—then we may be able to meet here again in five years' time and celebrate in 1948 the year of the beginning of world freedom. This would be exactly one hundred years after the year 1848, the tragic year of Europe, when freedom was driven from Germany and tens of thousands of her best citizens became exiles to America. If 1848 had been a year of victory for freedom, the wars of 1870, 1914, and 1939 might have been avoided. So dearly the world is now paying for this defeat of 1848.

With freedom established in 1948, we ourselves, our children, and our children's children will live in peace. Therefore, for the happiness of our children, let us put this figure "1948" in front of our writing tables, conference rooms, and churches. The year 1948 has to be the graduation year of all of us. But in the meantime we have

218

to learn some hard lessons. These are some of the lessons we have to learn:

1. World order or world disorder is a product of order or disorder in human character. If we wish a better world order, we have first to build an abundance of strong human characters.

2. This process of building such new characters has already begun among many who are suffering in combat zones, war-stricken areas, concentration camps, torture chambers, and underground movements. There freedom's army is being prepared. Those men and women are the mighty force to lead us all. We have to follow.

3. The best leaders among youth in all countries are burning in the desire to offer service and sacrifice in post-war reconstruction. Only if we offer to such youth an active part in reconstruction work and planning will we win peace, for a constructive peace can be won only if youth is on our side.

4. The abundance of food and fiber given by God to some countries needs to be directed and distributed as a stream of fresh water in the growing dry desert of distress and desperation of so many other countries. The irrigation effect, so well known in this nation, can be achieved on the moral field. Gardens of happiness and content will grow where there was death before. The tendency of the world toward growing deserts of war and desperation will change into the tendency toward growing gardens of peace.

5. On the cornerstones of these four bases the new building of a highly intensified education, full of a truly democratic spirit, can grow. It has to grow simultaneously throughout the world. If we fail in these four fields, even the best intentions and plans of educational reconstruction will be contradicted by our own failures, and the slow and modest way of recovery will become even slower.

I

Human character is the source of world order or world disorder. The very day when Mr. Wallace told us that the Germans by blood are neither better nor worse than other nations, but that textbooks and schoolmaster have had a deeper and more disastrous effect than ammunition and captains, a strange and horrible illustration appeared in the newspapers. In it we saw a picture of Kharkov after liberation by the victorious Russian armies. But six men could not enjoy the victory. They hung as corpses from the balcony of a school. Looking at this picture, I suddenly saw twelve dead men: six Russians, dead in body, but alive as martyrs; and the six German soldiers who were the hangmen. They may still be alive in body, but certainly their souls and minds are dead. Who killed the souls of those six German hangmen, and of millions and millions of pure, fine, decent German youth? The formula of the millstone around the neck may seem to many the only possible answer, and in this we can share the deep and profound anger with Jesus, the man of peace.

Grundtvig, the man who made the new Denmark, predicted more than a hundred years ago that the Germans would kill themselves. He did not say they would kill themselves by war or revolution or suicide. He predicted that they would kill themselves by their education. After 1819, under Metternich's influence, Prussia, the neighbor of Denmark, had broken away from liberal education and from Pestalozzi and his truly religious educational concept, and had started the sinister march toward death which we now see so evident. Three main errors Grundtvig mentioned. He said, first, that the German schools, the German learned schools, were educating youth in the spirit of a gang of Roman warriors who believe that the whole rest of the world lives but to serve them, to be dominated by them.

Secondly, he said, those boys were educated never to touch anything like a hammer or a spade or any other tool. The world of labor, of the toiling man, did not exist for them. And thirdly, he said, it was a doctrine of those German schools that life can be directed and formed from books and book knowledge only, without any practical life experience.

Today we see what those black schools leading toward death have produced; we see how the proud tower of Babylon with the swastika on top begins to crumble and to crack. Wait, and you will see more!

Friedrich Nietzsche, when he was professor in Basel in 1872, warned his Swiss friends in a similar way. He said that the system of German higher education, so highly praised in so many parts of the world, was producing a mass of half-educated barbarians whose only motivation was self-interest, aggressiveness, and urge for domination. One day the world would see what a danger had grown there. We see it now!

Denmark and Switzerland learned that education without the formation of strong and truly democratic character is a most dangerous and pernicious process. Others have learned the same lesson. Queen Wilhelmina of Holland, a great educator herself, learned it in 1919, and changed the Dutch educational system into a true democracy with full right of self-administration, even in religious matters. And England has shown her great and surprising power of resistance against aggression because for more than twenty years the new mass education system has highly developed the growth of truly democratic character in youth. And Russia has broken resolutely away from the rule of dry intellectualism in education and is offering to all classes a new, practical education system which proves today one of the great successes of our time. Just look at the high efficiency of the Russian soldier, farmer, and worker, all together the product of this new educational system. Today those millions move like a wall of steel against the barbarian aggression of those Nazi soldiers educated into abstract Frankensteins of destruction, ready to commit every crime and to explain and excuse every single action, even the worst crimes, by expediency, national duty, or some psychoanalytical tricks.

This is our present world crisis. We have abundance of scientific knowledge, technical machinery, production. We could feed, clothe, and make happy twice the population of most countries. But the one thing which by its very nature is outside the realm of science, human character, has been forgotten and neglected in some countries.

A skyscraper as a cardboard model and a skyscraper in life may have the same form, color, and plan; yet the cardboard model can easily stand anywhere, even on sand, while the skyscraper in life needs a stronger foundation. If built without this foundation, it cracks and crumbles in its very structure.

Cracking and crumbling is in many countries the proud structure of the bigger and better world order that man has planned and constructed in the last decades. Later generations, looking back with a deeper insight on our present world crisis, will discover that those countries attempted to build a gigantic skyscraper, scientifically correct, well planned and conceived, but set on a weak foundation. We forgot the old wisdom, "For every step forward in human civilization, human character should take two steps forward." But human character has had the opposite tendency. It has become weaker and weaker; and therefore perfect blueprints and plans, when applied to life, could not endure.

Postwar times and an effective new world order will make even more complicated national and international institutions necessary and inevitable. If they are again planned and conceived on the stage of cardboard models and blueprints only, without creating and developing at the same time human characters of an exceptionally high quality—men and women with a deep inner unselfishness and sense of national and world obligation—the world crisis will move from this scene to the next with increased momentum. The end of the fighting will mean not peace, but a breathing spell only.

Religion in past ages was one of the efficient processes developing human character strong enough to forget the motivation of selfishness and act on a larger concept. Historically the whole structure of Western education, social welfare, nursing, and the concept of equality, freedom, and the rights of man has developed first in strong religious characters, and from them has been able to live on. Religious characters still were developing some new educational and social concepts in the nineteenth century. Are religious characters no longer strong enough to master the larger concepts of the present world crisis? If this is true, man has arrived at the crossroad between disaster and hope, and the road sign points toward disaster rather than hope.

Can religion still act with speed and high efficiency to strengthen a sufficient number of religious characters to make a realistic, a large, a strong enough contribution toward the practical solution of the urgent world problems? Can religion for some years forget differentiations and divisions and act unitedly, as the priest acts on the battlefield, advising, strengthening, comforting all without distinction?

The human race as a whole is suffering on a large battlefield, a growing battlefield, even though its horrors have not yet reached some countries. The end of the fighting will not mean the end of that battlefield, for the military struggle

223

is only one part of the greater struggle going through the world. Killing of man and masses of men, devastation of property, families, and happiness, destruction of what man has built, go on inside and outside the military combat zone. To bring man back from this struggle of destruction and devastation is our task, and for this purpose more than victory is needed.

New men are needed for a new world. Without these new men the blueprints, the plans, of a new world are cardboard models only—perhaps beautiful models, well conceived, even perfect, but they will remain unreal if man remains inadequate to the new social and international obligations of the future.

Humanity indeed is preparing for its greatest trial. The spiritual forces and the deepest motivations of life are tested for success or failure.

II

But there is bright hope. This process of building such new characters has already begun in combat zones, war-stricken areas, concentration camps, in torture chambers and underground movements. There freedom's new army is in preparation. Those men and women are the mighty force to lead us. We have to follow.

This is nothing new. Europe, well experienced—what a bitter experience!—in postwar misery, knows well that some of the greatest personalities in the educational field, in the social field, have developed in such periods.

Grundtvig knew those forces very well and built on their foundation his whole formula and pattern to make a new world through new men. In his twenties, having passed through war, he grew depressed and desperate, as so many young religious persons do, about the decay of religion from an active, dynamic force to a bureaucratic institution and a "dead letter" only. He worried deeply about what he called "the withering away of the cross." Then suddenly in the darkness of his desperation came a revelation; an inner voice began to speak these prophetic words: "Every loss of a nation in its exterior structure can be compensated by strengthening the inner forces." So he aimed at making those inner forces of faith, kindness, tolerance, and co-operation, of skill, gardening, farm work, production, learning, of singing, dancing, and family life stronger and stronger. He connected all these single functions of the life of a nation to the service to the earth, to the crafts, to self-help and co-operative efforts. He used as an instrument what he called "the living word." He awakened in a world of dead-tired intellectualism the inspiration of teaching, the inspiration of songs, the inspiration of the best possible manual labor; and so he created Denmark anew, Denmark today, a small power in numbers of population, a big power in inner achievements, a modern power throughout the world. So this restless youth, disliking church fervently, was, when he died at eighty-nine, the most adored bishop of the reborn Danish church.

His educational formula was strange and surprising. In a time when book learning and examinations, imported from German school tradition, were everything, he hated mechanical book learning and was set against every form of examination. When everyone else liked to keep youth longer and longer in school, he proposed they should go into "the best school for adolescence": active life, productive skill, labor together with good, serious, hard-working farmers and craftsmen. He knew what he did in taking the compulsion to memorize and dislike books from the mind of the adolescent in those difficult years of transition, the adolescent years—as the French call them, "*l'age ingrat.*"

After five, six, or seven years in life work, the young

225

people came back in thousands into his new people's colleges. They became deeply devoted to learning, and developed into the best students and leaders in Europe—the Danish farmers. He made the farm land, the family home, and the community the centers of reconstruction. He believed so strongly in the inner forces and "the living word" that he did not permit any of his students even to take notes. "Forget what can be forgotten," he said; "the word which has touched your heart will come back alive at the right moment."

"But how?" a young farmer asked one of his teachers. Answered he, "Look, Jens, you put drain pipes in your farm land, and you need little sticks to put in the soil to find out where those pipes are." "Yes," said Jens. "But when you sow rye seeds in your farm land, do you put near every seed a little stick to find out where it lies?" "No," said Jens. "Why not?" the teacher asked. Jens replied, "They come to life and light by their own inner force." "The same," the teacher added, "is true with every word. If it is a living word, if it takes to your heart, forget it in your brain, for your heart will bring it to life at the right time."

From that light, from those inner forces, from those living words, Denmark lives today, even against Hitler.

Postwar times are the classical times when those inner forces come to new life. Leo Tolstoy in his great classical book *War and Peace*—call it the textbook of postwar reconstruction—speaks again and again about those strong inner forces. The tale of Moscow in October, 1812, is one of his great stories. Napoleon left Moscow devastated as Hitler's barbarous aggressors have left Stalingrad. "The place that has been known as Moscow," Tolstoy calls it, and he finds that in this place of ruins something indestructible and immaterial remained.

Those hundreds of thousands persecuted in Nazi Ger-

226

many during the last ten years inside and outside the concentration camps know this secret. When, protected and even encouraged by blind leaders of blind groups throughout the world, the Axis went on, invading, aggressing, destroying, hating, punishing, and mutilating everywhere, everywhere, they did not break down the inner resistance, the secret inner forces. Those forces will stand ready as soon as a sound and creative plan of reconstruction, sponsored by those of sincere religious motivation, is offered to those countries—a plan in which the main emphasis is put on self-help and co-operative efforts, a plan in which relief, raw materials, and credit are offered only as an encouragement to self-help.

Benedict of Nursia knew the secret of these inner, immaterial, but mighty forces; so he preached in a world devastated and degenerated by war his great message of the new order, the most humble order, the order of the living word of prayer and of manual labor. St. Francis knew it. Pestalozzi knew it. Fellenberg knew it. Ligthard knew it. And certainly the poet Charles Péguy knew it when he died on the battlefield in 1914, leaving his message to all those millions who regard him today as their great friend and teacher, sending his message to all those whom he called blessed because they died, in obedience and humility, in a just war.

Blessed are those who died defending their hearths and its fire
And the poor honor of their fathers' houses;
For such houses are the image and the beginning,
And the body and the attempt of the House of God.

What are these invisible but mighty inner forces? Let us turn to Tolstoy for an explanation of the secret. On the same pages where he writes about Moscow he speaks about something he likes even more than Moscow—the

Russian man, represented in Pierre, this charming, delightful young Russian, so typical in all of his style of living, acting, and reacting. Let us look at Pierre. Now at the end of the war, after the victory of 1812, when reconstruction begins, when a new world will be established, he finds himself an entirely changed man. He discovers to his great surprise "new thoughts within him which he could apply in any question. He had no more doubts or hesitations." Now there is "a judge within him, settling what he must do and what he must not do by some laws of which he was himself unaware." He makes straightforward, clear, and simple decisions. He recognizes in the new life within him the right solutions, and he settles his personal relationships, the rebuilding of his houses in Moscow, and all other questions in a new and better way. In discussions he takes strongly the part of Russian youth which from the beginning of the nineteenth century took part in the great dream of European youth that one day, as Schiller said, the governments of nations would be formed on a new basis, taking the great experience of friendship as its motto and granting to all freedom of thought.

This first freedom, freedom of thought, was considered in those years of the beginning of the youth renaissance throughout Europe and America as the foundation of all other freedoms.

Another young man of these first decades of the nineteenth century, transformed by the bitter experience of war, of a lost war, of suppression and exile, wrote a beautiful interpretation of this great aim of the youth renaissance throughout Europe. From the pen of the great Polish poet Mickiewicz came this ode to youth:

Without heart, without soul, peoples of the world are skeletons only. Oh, youth and friends, everywhere bring from the sphere of visions and ideals down to earth a new world. Oh, youth and friends, sweetness of life is not sweet at all, if it is not shared. Together, youth, go together, win over the egotists and force the world to leave the dead tracks of the past, the ice of the prejudices breaks; welcome dawning glory of freedom, after you the sun will come. Together, youth, together.

"Sweetness of life is not sweet at all, if it is not shared." The difficult task of reconstruction in all war-stricken countries may be surprisingly easy and not too complicated at all under one condition—under the condition that we all together enroll in this yet unseen but mighty army of those who have been passing through the great hardships of the fight against Nazism and the barbarous Axis philosophy, of those who regard the loss of all their belongings, of their friends and families, and the daily danger of life as a small price for this one greatest of all goods, freedom. Those who never, never, and never had any share with Hitler's pagan forces of destruction, never sat down at the same table to wine and dine with the Nazis—they will make their greatest contribution to the reconstruction of Europe and Asia because they are ready to sacrifice everything. "He that loseth his life . . . . shall find it."

Believe me, those who know this inner structure of Europe and Asia feel sometimes inclined to give encouragement to those who try to solve those problems in terms of facts and figures, statistics, raw materials, food, and textiles only. Those who know the inner forces are convinced that all material, financial, and personal effort from the outside can be cut in half or less if only those millions who resisted aggression, those fighters against Nazism, can be united in one great plan of mutual self-help and constructive co-operation. But if those forces are not enlisted,

229

or even not invited, and from a different aspect of life without these new experiences an attempt is made to reconstruct the world, then it may be a very different, even most difficult, situation.

So we come to the conclusion that the first great preparation of human character for a new world order has begun without, even against, man's intention; but those who know this mighty and indestructible power behind history as Tolstoy knew it are not surprised to find that in our time this power has again come into the hearts of men. We may find one day that nine tenths of the process of creating the new human character—fitted, hardened, shaped, and reborn for those great tasks ahead of us—is done on the battlefields of Europe and Asia, in the concentration camps and torture chambers. Wherever Nazi and Axis brutality hits hard, there the spark of a new life springs ahead, like Athene from the head of Zeus. All we have to do is to accept these facts and to recognize these new men and women for what they really are, our guides to follow.

III

But a second arsenal of new human character is at our hand, abundantly ready, if we only will not spoil this arsenal but use its forces for the purpose for which it was created. Youth, the best of our young people everywhere, is burning, more or less openly, in a fire of devotion for a great cause, known or unknown, until we, the older people, by our skepticism extinguish the fire.

Everyone who has been favored with the confidence of youth in many countries knows this deep inner devotion of youth. If they speak openly, directly, without an attempt to hide the best in their minds, then young men and women in all continents and countries speak exactly like those young poets and leaders of other decades: "Sweetness of life is not sweet at all, if it is not shared"; "Every loss of a nation . . . . can be compensated by strengthening the inner forces"; "An inner voice tells me in danger exactly what to do"; "Blessed are those who died defending their hearths and its fire and . . . . the image and the beginning . . . . of the House of God."

There will be many Grundtvigs and Tolstoys and Mickiewiczes, and perhaps even a Charles Péguy—"our dear Péguy," as Herriot says—waiting in the dark; and they will appear if we welcome them, encourage them, or they will remain silent if the world is too hard and unkind against them.

For many years youth in all countries of the United Nations has been fervently interested in the problems of a new world order. This dream of a new world order is so much a basic concept of youth that everyone who attempted to build his power on youth support, even Hitler himself, had to include the essentials of this concept in his written program, in his speeches. The day when youth discovers that Hitler has broken his promise, then youth will abandon him in masses.

Mickiewicz stated one part of this youth dream: "Sweetness of life is not sweet at all, if it is not shared." That means, applied to the life interest of youth: equality of educational opportunity for all youth; full employment of all who can work; great social institutions fully protecting the security of the child, the aged, and the sick. These are some of the elements of this new dream of youth.

This dream has now passed from the abstract to the concrete. Throughout Europe and Asia, in all countries invaded by Hitler or the Japanese, the aggressors did not find any support from youth. Youth in all those invaded countries and in England defends this dream with the lives of tens of thousands of martyrs against those barbarous suppressors; and among those martyrs are numerous religious leaders, workers, farmers, teachers, professors, and pupils. This wave of persecution of the true youth leaders, the attempt to eliminate them in any case from the future scene, takes place inside and outside Germany. The reports about those unspeakable horrors of killing and torturing in Central and Eastern Europe and in Russia are well known. A new report has come through that in certain parts of Germany 90 per cent of all members of the Catholic and Protestant youth organizations are now killed. They report that in the battle of Stalingrad at the most dangerous point a death battalion was put in action which was entirely annihilated. This battalion comprised, among others, 250 young Protestant ministers and Catholic priests. They died according to Hitler's wishes together with their friends and companions.

In this policy of taking out of the European and Asiatic space those religious and intellectual forces that could be of the greatest help in the postwar time, Hitler reveals his true character, which is not atheistic only, but dynamically antitheistic. At the same time that he destroys young leaders in all invaded countries, from Holland and France to the Russian plains, from the North to Greece, he maintains and protects in most elaborate youth camps in Germany many thousands of young Guard and Gestapo students who are trained in the most careful system to be one day, under democratic disguise, under religious disguise, ready to offer their services in the reconstruction throughout the world, proceeding with one great formula in their minds: "to disseminate distrust, uneasiness, and disunity among the United Nations, and to make the work of reconstruction as difficult as possible." For Hitler, too, has

232

his postwar plans, even for the possibility that he will lose his first war now and enter an armistice called peace.

But youth throughout Europe will not forget that those who died as martyrs for the great cause of defending freedom of thought, freedom of faith, have put a mission in the hearts of those who survive; and whenever martyrs have been the seeds of a new church, then throughout Europe a new union of dynamic and constructive faith will grow. The message of these martyrs will be that everyone who enrolls in any official and organized group activity of reconstruction accepts these hard postwar years ready to forget difficulties, to forget even self-interest of the organization, to work shoulder to shoulder, peaceful together with all who are waiting to build on the plan of those youth visions the firm structure of a new union of the peaceful nations throughout the world. Not only does this dream of serving the coming better world exist in the war-stricken countries; the desire to take an active part in reconstruction and in all other responsibilities and to make postwar plans together with the adults exists to the same degree here in America. Many of these young people have expressed their hope that one day no meeting of any responsible group in the field of reconstruction will take place in which a large number of young people are not fully represented with the same right to express their opinions and intentions as the older people.

At the same time, when millions of boys are called to die on the battlefield, we should give to youth the right of full participation in all those efforts in planning. It may even be time to consider giving these young people a full share in all councils of community, religious and nonreligious, which are steering the welfare of all and planning the better well-being of the future. From personal experiences through many years I may state that those young

233

people will pay back such a confidence with sincere and genuine devotion.

IV

The fourth lesson we have to learn, before we can be ready to consider the postwar world peacefully established and freedom on its way, is the task to share the postwar abundance of food and fiber with the poorer and suffering countries and to make their desert of desperation into a field from which, by their own intensive effort, a garden of peace and happiness can grow.

In going year after year through most countries of Europe, studying the movements of youth, underground and open, I have discovered that no other single factor has caused more bitter feeling and desperation among youth than the fact that in a world of abundance poverty and unemployment prevail. That in Argentina, Brazil, Canada, and America, corn, wheat, and cotton were destroyed; in Denmark, cows, and in France, fishes and wines. That in all those countries artificial limitations of production were imposed and at the same time millions and millions in Europe lived in dire misery. Children died in hunger, the eyes of mothers were full of tears, and the foreheads of fathers were heavy with desperation because there was no work, no bread, no farming. The cycles of unemployment grew higher and higher, and more and more vigorous, and the best goods of the world were destroyed.

In analyzing why so many churches and religious organizations in Europe lost their most important members—youth—I discovered again and again that this crime of prewar times, the crime of neglect and omission, of misery and unemployment in a world of abundance, was the cause. I remember that one day one of the leading Catholic priests of Paris in an international meeting firmly attacked the interpretation that the restlessness of youth was caused by Communist agitators. "No," he said, "this restlessness, bitterness, and desperation is caused by our own short-comings, errors, and mistakes. God made the world abundant, and man made it miserable. God intended everyone to be happy, and man created unhappiness and desperation without limitation."

Every one of us should train his thoughts to accept and to repeat this simple new fact. During the last few decades the most fundamental change in human history has taken place. Before this change, hunger in certain parts of the world, undernourishment by lack of food, disaster by lack of transportation, were inevitable. During the last few decades God has given into the brains of scientists and the skilled hands of the farmers, engineers, and technicians the power, the miracle, of feeding the multitudes. Where God has given such power into man's hand, man should act and not wait for another miracle.

Up till some decades ago Malthus was right in stating that humanity expanded faster than the space to produce sufficient food and fiber for all. Now Malthus has been contradicted by Wallace, Wickard, and the force of American mass production. All Americans should be extremely proud to know that this magnificent institution of the American farm organization produced in 1942, in addition to all other war efforts, enough food to feed twenty million more human beings. The miracle in man's hands!

When the war effort ceases, the last shot is fired, the last enemy is conquered, then suddenly this tremendous machine of production will be slowing its speed, decreasing its capacity, waning again. Hundreds of thousands who are willing to serve with all their skills will fear unemployment; and in spite of such possible reductions, the great powerhouse of food and raw materials, the Americas, will be full to the bursting point while in Europe and Asia millions will be hungry, miserable, underfed, dying. There will be in our hands wheat, corn, cotton, and wool—all fiber needed for clothing—coffee, sugar, milk, and honey in abundance. And this great abundance of milk and honey should call back to our minds some great examples of abundance before. In those old bygone times, when history served coming generations still as a lesson in human character, Moses reported three cases of abundance unlimited: Paradise was abundant with food and everything needed for life; the great plains before the flood were full of abundance, with people forgetting the misery of others and being inclined in their saturated life to violence; and the big towns of Sodom and Gomorrah had no misery and poverty, but abundance all around. Moses tells us the story that all these three examples of abundance were destroyed. Why? They were destroyed because man was not growing the same measure of abundance in the qualities that make men truly great—the qualities of sharing with others in distress, co-operation as far as the hand of man can reach, and encouragement of those who are weak to become strong, skillful, and self-sufficient.

We are approaching a new situation of abundance. Here again are corn, wheat, fowl, cattle, cotton, wool, iron, steel, coal, coffee, tea, honey, and milk in abundance; and yet if we do not learn this lesson, again this sweetness of life will become bitter if it is not shared.

To repeat, perhaps the greatest lesson we have to learn in our time is the lesson that every step forward in scientific and technical development should be accompanied by at least two steps forward in the moral and spiritual perfection of man. The more power and abundance is given into the hand of man, the more we should be ready to follow the one way that takes man to the climax of creation—the willingness to help and to share. In China, we are told, they call it "the Jesus Way." In other countries, they use other words, or do it silently.

V

We approach now the field on which the most difficult problem of postwar times has to be solved. To overcome the hardship of this period, and to prevent the recurrence of a new war, we need a highly efficient system of education, truly and effectively democratic in structure and aims, spreading slowly throughout the world, but beginning immediately inside the liberated Axis countries.

Postwar times are the right hour to change the bitter experience of human failure into the sweet fruit of human progress. Suffering always can become the beginning of such new steps forward. It can be a challenge to strengthen the inner forces against losses. In many fields of our international and national life such inner forces were absent or weak before, but such inner new forces of mind and soul are most urgently needed for the progress of humanity.

This philosophy of suffering will not be a strange philosophy for those who have gone in their thoughts with the multitude into the mountains to listen to the Man who came not to destroy but to fulfill, who invited us to answer misery with charity and loneliness with love and kindness, and who taught the people as one who had authority.

Without such authority nothing can be done in the whole field of education. Experience is not enough. Without such authority certainly nothing can be done to re-educate those who were educated in errors and to bring the right education to those many millions who had no education at all or a weak education only.

This is the wide field of educational reconstruction after this war. Certainly re-education of Nazi youth and Axis youth is most urgently needed, but all our efforts will be in vain and all our attempts to guide from the outside will be failures, if we do not lift the whole of education everywhere to a higher level, to better intellectual and moral standards.

A doctrine like Hitlerism can be overcome only by something stronger and more effective. No police force, no military occupation—authority is what is needed. Two other forces are needed: first, the force of a great plan and the vision to realize the concept of the Atlantic Charter effectively by education; and second, the force of the good will and confidence of those people inside the Axis countries who are truly democratic, including those millions of youth who, after the defeat of the Axis powers, will be deeply disappointed and eager to find a new concept of life. Democracy—world democracy—can be this concept, but only if the Atlantic Charter is realized and implemented everywhere around the earth, at least in the field of youth welfare and education.

Postwar times are critical times; and only what we *are*, not what we *say* and *intend*, has weight.

Now for the first time a leading statesman of the United Nations, Vice President Wallace, has called Germans with the right attitude to begin rewriting German textbooks; and he added that we shall need the help of all Germans who can give convincing evidence that they do not subscribe to the lies and crimes of Nazi teaching. At the same time he warned rightly against the great danger of a wrong emotionalism of "soft, lazy forgetfulness" which certainly again will be ready to forget and forgive everything and to make no moral discrimination at all. Such attempts will be made; they will weaken and contradict all those who have resisted so heroically.

As one of those who for more than fifteen years have

238

been preparing for the day when after Hitler's defeat we should be called upon to make a contribution to re-education throughout Europe, I should like to thank Vice President Wallace for those statements, and I should like to tell him that many of us are ready to do what he proposes. In fact, some of us have begun to write new textbooks and to prepare new plans and schemes for education. But if now the Vice President of the United States invites us to do more, then we can do more, and we will do more. His words will one day be regarded as the beginning of a charter of co-operation between Europe and America in the field of educational reconstruction.

When Hitler is beaten and our many friends of truly democratic attitude and strong anti-Nazi feeling can come out all over Europe from the concentration camps, prisons, or other hiding places, the world will see that among these people are some of the strongest and most reliable fighters for freedom and democratic education. They know no compromises because for so long they have looked the enemy in the eye and learned that every slightest compromise means moral defeat.

But all of those who will be called to establish democratic education throughout Europe and prevent the recurrence of barbarism will be much too weak unless from the outside a strong, powerful authority supports the same efforts in the same direction. If again, as in 1919, isolationism rules in the field of international education—or opposing tendencies are not only ignored but even supported, as happened so often in the beginning of Nazism—then all efforts will be lost.

What we need is close co-operation with a high, moral international authority standing for the same principles of democratic education everywhere.

In the darkest hours of Europe, when Napoleon's tyranny had crushed even Swiss freedom and made the Swiss Republic a vassal state, Pestalozzi made the statement that the cause of this decline was that Europe had no father. Between 1919 and 1939, Europe indeed had no father; no great authority existed which in a friendly or hard way could have warned us and the world against the crimes of Nazism in the field of education. Could Europe have had such a great authority, many of the crimes of Nazism in the field of youth and education would have been prevented.

Now is the time to establish such a great authority, a moral and intellectual authority. We do not need to speak in mystical or symbolical terms any longer. We are asking for and proposing an International Education Office, and behind it a great International Education Organization, in which, beside the selected representatives of educators, governments, parents, and youth of all nations, the most highly respected personalities of international reputation shall protect and direct education throughout the world. This organization should act as if the full power of a world government, which will come one day, were already existing.

But certainly such an office should in no way centralize education; on the contrary, it should promote decentralized education, adapted to the federal principle.

As model we claim the International Labor Office and the International Labor Organization, which have done so much to raise the standards of labor throughout the world and to promote international good will and co-operation.

But the International Education Office should be, even in a higher degree than the International Labor Office, a high moral authority with autonomy in all questions of approving or disapproving textbooks, tendencies, and philosophies of education. Its aim should be to raise everywhere truly democratic principles, and for this purpose to counsel, guide, promote, and direct the democratization of education in all countries. A number of first-rate experts from the most advanced countries should be at the disposal of this International Education Office. Whenever this Office should discover somewhere tendencies like those promoted by the Axis countries—tendencies fostering hatred, aggressiveness, and immoral concepts—then this authority, like a father, should not hesitate to warn, and even to invite the other nations to take action and stop any non-co-operation, perhaps even take more drastic steps, until the democratic minority in such a country strengthened by this support, should become again a majority and be able itself to take care of the situation.

For more than fifteen years the different groups in Europe who are prepared for educational reconstruction after Hitler's defeat have been preparing such plans. In England such plans have been prepared for years. The United States Committee on Educational Reconstruction took up such plans a long time ago. A special commission has prepared the beginning of concrete proposals; and we intend in a few weeks time, when we meet with our friends from the Central and Eastern European countries for a two-day Institute on Educational Reconstruction, to propose a concrete plan, together with a charter of democratic education, which we hope one day will be accepted throughout the world.

But we certainly have no intention to pretend that these ideas are ours. Every student of the history of education knows that such plans have existed for more than three hundred years. Comenius dreamed of what he called a "House of Solomon." Shortly afterward, plans for an "International University" with similar functions were proposed in other parts of Europe. Condorcet, Pestalozzi, and

Fellenberg dreamed about some kind of *"sittlichen Mensch-enverein,"* a moral union of Humanism; Jullien developed such plans; but the honor of having made the most concrete preparation is due to an American woman, Mrs. F. Fern Andrews. In 1912 she succeeded in arranging for the Queen of Holland to invite sixteen governments to Holland to form an International Education Office. Fifteen governments accepted; one refused—Germany. Before the conference—set for September 1, 1914—could start, the World War came and ended this dream. The Peace Conference took it up again, but the Counsel of Ten killed the plan. All that came out of it was a more or less nonofficial International Bureau of Education in Geneva, not a part of the League of Nations, but developed under the three great international educators, M. Piaget, Miss Butts, and M. Rosello, into a very important agency for research and exchange of experiences. This bureau, which was supported by a number of governments, certainly will be a part, may be even a nucleus, of any new scheme.

The significance of the International Education Office will depend upon the International Charter of Education which may be adopted by it and by all member states as an expression of its guiding principles, to be realized with speed, but taking the conditions of every nation into consideration. India, for example, certainly will need much more time; yet her effort to achieve democratic education for all should make her eligible not only for full membership, but we hope for more. We hope that inside this new International Education Organization a world brotherhood develops, saying: "What is mine shall be yours. Here are all my experiences and resources of international good will, all my best experts and training centers; India, dear sister India, make use of them." And we know that the people in England, and especially youth throughout

242

England, will be the first to say so. When this happens, educational reconstruction will have two meanings: man will be educated; so will international institutions.

There is not yet any official text or even draft ready for this International Charter of Education. Everyone can therefore now attempt to be among the legislators and writers—or shall we say prophets?—of such a charter. The following points are such an attempt. They are addressed to all who believe in the words of Jesus, or of the old prophets of Israel, that justice and love shall fill the earth. They are aiming at the purpose of forming a common charter for all, without mentioning the spiritual or religious issues, as for such issues every group and church may rightly have its own plans and intentions. They intend to be a *minima regula humana*—a minimum charter of youth and welfare and education in general, in the best sense of the word "humanism." All who believe in such a goal can unite in such a charter.

It is proposed, then, to—

1. Protect the mind and soul of every child and youth against the crime of moral and intellectual mutilation, as every human tradition protects the child against murder. To murder mind and soul is worse than to murder the body.
2. Protect the body and life of every child and youth against suffering hunger, misery, and destitution. To the child and the youth, as the first citizens of the world, abundance of goods shall first be directed.
3. Offer to every youth up to the stage of adolescence full, free basic education, skill-training, and formation of character as a good neighbor and citizen—this to be compulsory for all.
4. Offer to all adolescents and adults the free opportunity, according to their own will and capacity, to perfect themselves permanently in intelligence, art, skill, and good citi-

zenship. Life work and learning should be closely interconnected.

5. In all these questions let self-responsibility and self-help be the first rule and guiding principle. Where self-help fails, the family should step in; where the family fails, the local community; where the local community fails, the province or state; after this the nation, the neighboring group of nations, and at the end the world community. Every help from the larger unit should be directed toward making the smaller unit fully effective again. What anyone can do for himself no one should do for him.

6. In all these matters let complete equality of opportunity rule without any discrimination in questions of sex, race, class, or creed. As soon as a talent is discovered, such talent should be promoted and supported until the highest development of the person's special gifts are reached. Society has nothing more important and rarer than true talents.

7. Lift the standards and the standing of the educator everywhere. Invite and select for this great public function of education the best of youth. Give to the educators, who have to speak for humanity and justice, such independence and security that they can fulfill their function courageously and without fear. Give them all chances to remain fresh, well informed, and better and better prepared; their task is to form a fresher, better, and more informed citizenship of the future.

8. Bring to youth moral and spiritual values. Replace the motivation of self-interest and expediency by reverence and devotion toward great ideals and aims. Develop the co-operative spirit in small and large groups. Give to youth the chance of participating in public tasks according to capacity. Develop everywhere hand and brain together.

9. Strengthen loyalty toward family, community, and nation, but direct all visions and actions toward the realization of the brotherhood of man. Only the peace that we create

244

by our own action can fill international relations and treaties with full life.

10. To promote these plans, create an International Education Office in which the best experts in every important field of education shall be called together to promote the best ways and means of expanding the democratic character of education in all countries. In the permanent council give a permanent seat to a number of the most highly respected leaders of the nations, persons who have excelled in learning, art, philosophy, social work, and statesmanship—these, once appointed, to select their own successors. Invite every educator and every youth throughout the world to co-operate in some fields actively. Youth movements devoted to the service of community should be directly connected with this office, which should maintain a special training center and college for the education of future leaders in international co-operation and close relations between the educational systems. The main task of the International Education Office should be to improve and increase permanently the intellectual, moral, technical, and artistic qualities of learning everywhere, and to develop effective methods of self-help and co-operation. The textbooks and teaching methods should be continually investigated; and every danger of undemocratic or aggressive tendencies, endangering the peace inside or between the nations, should be immediately met with the appropriate steps. In times of crisis, the International Education Office should be the agency through which the other nations extend help to the suffering nations. These may repay later on, so that such relief and support can be made available to others.

Two examples may show how such an International Education Office would deal with a difficult situation: the case of Germany, and the case of those countries in which the Germans have systematically destroyed the institutions and the personnel of education.

245

In the case of Germany such an office would call together at an early moment the best experts of true democratic character. All of the most important anti-Nazi groups would be represented. With those men and women of German or other origin this office would prepare plans to re-educate Nazi youth and bring the older generation back to an understanding of the ways of democracy. Textbooks would be prepared, and the demand for new teachers would be investigated. Appropriate steps would be taken to prepare as many democratic teachers as possible to serve, immediately after the downfall of Hitler, as advisers and experts for the training of new teachers from the ranks and files of the anti-Nazi opposition. The population inside Germany would be informed by regular broadcasts, so that the older generation would know now that the most urgent question can be solved—how to bring youth back to democratic ideals, back to the families, and back to learning. Such preparations would help in a very high degree to make the anti-Nazi opposition in Germany ready for resistance and for hope that Hitler's defeat will not mean the annihilation of the whole of Germany.

In the case of the Nazi-invaded countries, the office would establish close co-operation with the governments in exile and the refugee scholars and teachers. Week after week a register would be compiled of what institutions of learning and schools are destroyed and how many teachers, educators, and scholars are killed. This information would be announced regularly to the whole world of education. The Nazis would be told: "The more you destroy the more we will rebuild. You, the Nazis, consider those nations as the most hated nations; we consider them from now on in all our effots as the most favored nations, and we will not rest before everything you destroyed is restored." Thousands of teachers and scholars would be in preparation; all material would be collected, so that from the day of liberation the active reconstruction could begin and the schools and colleges and universities could be reopened with speed.

All this sounds simple and natural, but we have to confess that very little is done in this direction, because there is no institution which can act in this field for the democratic nations of the world.

Omission in this field may have grave consequences and be very expensive. The rebuilding of democratic education in Axis countries and the reconstruction of education in the invaded countries, unless something is done immediately, may be largely improvised; and thousands and thousands of youth will suffer because we are not ready.

Still it is not too late. Every group should act, especially every religious group; for to work for those in distress, for those who suffer, is a natural duty of any true religious conviction. Cannot the religious leaders of all confessions and creeds come together and consider how they can promote actively such steps and call from among their younger members a pioneer group of action?

Someone was asked one day what the best textbook of religious teaching after the war in the war-stricken countries will be. He gave the answer that the best textbook will be the reports of what religious groups did in the field of general relief and support of those who suffered, especially outside their own ecclesiastical field—how they acted to help not only their own brothers in faith but also those who were just human beings in distress. Asked to imagine what such a textbook might report—what should be done—he wrote down, as if from a date in 1948, five years from now, the following account:

Looking at the great suffering of millions and millions in all lands, the religious leaders of many churches and temples came together in 1943 and decided to do the opposite of what Herod did to the Christ Child. They decided to protect, support, and help the child everywhere, silently and effectively, all together. They decided to work together like brothers and sisters, the sons and daughters of one father. They solemnly resolved not to use this pioneer work for the purpose of winning new members for any particular church group.

Looking at the endless misery of the world they decided to forget for five years all differences and to work silently as servants of the great dynamic forces which some call God, and others feel as the great mysterious power that suddenly "warmeth thy heart from the inside" before words or ideologies can intervene. During all the years of reconstruction, no one did a better job, accomplished finer work, was more devoted and unselfish throughout the world, than these who called themselves the "New Pioneers of Humanity."

Such a textbook of postwar learning, showing how great man can grow, certainly is still a dream, a fiction. But who knows if somewhere in Europe or Asia, or elsewhere, some young courageous men and women will not form such a silent group of pioneers, acting quietly to save mankind —and religion.

If religion is expressed in actions and dynamic, unselfish personalities, then religion will be highly respected everywhere. One single St. Francis, or John Wesley, or Don Bosco, or Albert Schweitzer can today impress millions who are waiting exactly for this kind of powerful, dynamic expression of religion.

Religion, after many crises and errors, will return to the symbolic word of Comenius mentioned before: "Religion is not the picture of a growing tree, but the tree itself"—the tree itself, full of growing, silent strength, a living expression of the great, immaterial, but mighty and indestructible power behind history.

When a few weeks ago, for the first time after three years

248

of silence, the church bells of the English churches filled the air with their happy songs, glorifying the victory of the Eighth Army in Africa, and the sound of these old sweet, silvery bells of Coventry came through the air by short wave in my rooms, one strange word was spoken by the commentator to the jubilant melody of those sweet-singing bells. The commentator stood among the ruins of the town, greater than ever now, and he said these surprising words: "There is a strange power in ruins." Indeed, there is a strange power in ruins; and because we have passed through disaster and misery, because with us are those hundreds of thousands of martyrs who fight, who live in ruins, those in ruins will have found a new way of life.

What will we do? We, not in ruins, but still far away from bombing and distress, living in a country still in abundance? Upon our answer to this question the new world throughout all five continents may depend.

BIOGRAPHICAL NOTES

HENRY A. WALLACE

BORN and reared in the Iowa farm country, Mr. Wallace studied agriculture at Iowa State College (B.S. and honorary M.S.) and was for many years editor of *Wallaces' Farmer*, both before and after its merger with *Iowa Homestead*. He was Secretary of Agriculture of the United States from March 4, 1933, until his nomination for Vice President in 1940. He is author of a number of books on agriculture and political affairs, of which recent titles are *The American Choice* (1940) and *The Price of Free World Victory* (1942).

FRANCIS J. McCONNELL

BISHOP McCONNELL was educated at Ohio Wesleyan University (A.B.) and Boston University (S.T.B., Ph.D.) and has received honorary degrees from a number of universities. After pastorates in New England and New York, he was president of DePauw University from 1909 till his election to the episcopacy in 1912. As bishop he has served the Methodist Areas of Denver, Pittsburgh, and, since 1928, New York. He has been president of the Religious Education Association, the Federal Council of the Churches of Christ in America, and the American Association for Social Security. Beside being Lyman Beecher lecturer at Yale in 1930, Barrows lecturer in India in 1931, and Drew lecturer in biography in 1942, Bishop McConnell is now for the third time a Merrick lecturer, having delivered the series in 1912 and the opening lecture of the 1942 series. His books include a number of volumes on the philosophy of religion and the application of Christianity to the social problems of the day, and more recently the biography *John Wesley* (1939) and the Drew Lectures, *Evangelicals, Revolutionists and Idealists* (1942).

WILLIS J. KING

AFTER graduation from Wiley College (A.B.) in his native state of Texas, Dr. King continued his studies in Boston University (S.T.B., Ph.D.) and Harvard Divinity School. He served several pastorates and then became professor of Old Testament and Christian sociology at Gammon Theological Seminary. After two years as president of Samuel Huston College in Austin, Texas, he returned to Atlanta in 1932 to assume his present position as president of Gammon. In 1929-30 he was a fellow of the Julius Rosenwald Fund for research at Oxford University and in Palestine under the auspices of the American School of Oriental Re-

BIOGRAPHICAL NOTES

search. He represented Negro students at the World's Student Christian Federation in Peking, China, in 1922, and was a delegate to the Conference on Life and Work at Oxford in 1937. He is a member of the American Oriental Society, the Southern Sociological Society, and the Board of Directors of the Atlanta School of Social Work.

EDGAR S. BRIGHTMAN

DR. BRIGHTMAN has studied in Brown University (A.B., A.M.), Boston University (S.T.B., Ph.D.), and the Universities of Berlin and Marburg, Germany, and has been honored with degrees from other universities. After professorships in Nebraska Wesleyan University and Wesleyan University (Connecticut), he assumed in 1919 his present position as professor of philosophy in Boston University. He is a member of the American Philosophical Association, the Religious Education Association, the American Association of University Professors, and has been president of the American Theological Society and the National Association of Biblical Instructors. He has lectured at Harvard University, Lowell Institute, Duke University, the University of Michigan, and Vanderbilt University, and is author of numerous books in the field of philosophy, of which the latest are *A Philosophy of Religion* (1940) and his Cole Lectures at Vanderbilt, *The Spiritual Life* (1942).

UMPHREY LEE

A NATIVE of Indiana, Dr. Lee was educated at Trinity University in Texas (A.B.), Southern Methodist University (A.M.), Union Theological Seminary, and Columbia University (Ph.D.), and has received honorary degrees from other universities. After only a few years in the ministry he was appointed to the large Highland Park Methodist Church, Dallas, Texas, and was pastor there for over twelve years. During five years of this period he was at the same time professor of homiletics at Southern Methodist University. In 1936 he became dean of the School of Religion and professor of church history at Vanderbilt University, and in 1939 returned to Southern Methodist University to assume his present position as president. He is a member of the Mediaeval Academy of America and the Wesley Historical Society of England. His writings include several books on John Wesley and early Methodist history and *The Historic Church and Modern Pacifism*, just published.

GONZALO BÁEZ-CAMARGO

DR. CAMARGO was born in Oaxaca, Mexico, and was educated in the Normal School at Puebla and the Union Theological Seminary at Mexico City. He is a former professor and vice president of the Mexican Methodist Institute, Puebla. Beside being executive secretary of the

252

BIOGRAPHICAL NOTES

National Evangelical Council of Mexico, he is manager of the Union Publishing House in Mexico City. Among his writings are *Hacia la Renovación Religiosa en Hispanoamérica* (1933), *Principios y Método de la Educación Cristiana* (1933), and, with K. G. Grubb, *Religion in the Republic of Mexico* (1935).

JOHN B. CONDLIFFE

DR. CONDLIFFE was born in Australia and studied at Canterbury College of the University of New Zealand (M.A., D.Sc.), with later reading and research in Gonville and Caius College, Cambridge, England. After some years as professor of economics at Canterbury College and then as research secretary of the Institute of Pacific Relations, he came to the United States as visiting professor of economics at the University of Michigan for the year 1930-31. Thereafter he went to Europe to become a member of the Secretariat of the League of Nations and later professor of commerce at the University of London before returning to this country to assume his present position as professor of economics at the University of California in Berkeley. He is also rapporteur of the International Chamber of Commerce and International Studies Conference, and chairman of the International Research Committee of the Institute of Pacific Relations. He has written much on economics and international trade, particularly as regards countries in the Pacific area, recent books being *The Reconstruction of World Trade* (1940) and *Agenda for a Postwar World* (1942).

BJARNE BRAATOY

ALTHOUGH born in Minnesota, Dr. Braatoy moved in childhood to Norway. After two spells at sea, he undertook the study of law in the University of Oslo and completed the course after terms of special study in Berlin and Paris. Setting out to practice law in Oslo, he soon found that his abilities lay in the field of journalism and became a newspaper correspondent, working over a period of years in the principal capitals of Europe. Meanwhile he did reasearch in international affairs and studied further at the University of London (Ph.D.). As a lecturer on various aspects of international political and economic organization he spoke to audiences in most countries of Europe, and over the radio in London, Copenhagen, and New York. In 1940 he came to New York as public relations officer of the Norwegian Shipping and Trade Mission, and soon became also coeditor of *New Europe* and acting Norwegian representative on the Inter-Allied Information Committee. He has continued lecturing here, particularly for the Foreign Policy Association, and has taken part in a number of round-table broadcasts. He is now president of the League for Industrial Democracy. He was called to his present work with the Office of War Information last year.

BIOGRAPHICAL NOTES

VERA MICHELES DEAN

MRS. DEAN is a graduate of Radcliffe College, with a master's degree in international law from Yale University and a Ph.D. from Radcliffe. Since 1928 she has been a member of the research staff of the Foreign Policy Association, specializing in Russian and Italian affairs and problems of European diplomacy. She edits all the Association's research publications and has written many of them herself. Her most recent reports and pamphlets include *Toward a New World Order, European Agreements for Post-War Reconstruction, The Struggle for World Order, Russia at War*, and *What Future for Germany?*

CHARLES-EDWARD A. WINSLOW

AFTER his training at the Massachusetts Institute of Technology (B.S., M.S.), Yale University (A.M.), and New York University (Doctor of Public Health), Dr. Winslow taught biology and bacteriology at the Massachusetts Institute of Technology and the College of the City of New York, and in 1915 assumed his present position as professor of public health in the Yale Medical School. He was also curator of public health for the American Museum of Natural History, New York, from 1910 to 1922. In 1917 he was a member of the American Red Cross mission to Russia. For a time he was general medical director of the League of Red Cross Societies in Geneva, and later was for three years expert assessor of the Health Committee of the League of Nations. He has been a member of the board of scientific directors of the International Health Division of the Rockefeller Foundation and of the advisory council of the National Institute of Health, and has been president of the American Public Health Association and of the Society of American Biologists. Since 1938 he has been chairman of the Housing Authority of New Haven, Connecticut. His numerous writings in the field of public health include both reports of research and textbooks.

CARTER GOODRICH

BORN in New Jersey, the son of a minister, Dr. Goodrich was educated at Amherst College (A.B.) and the University of Chicago (Ph.D.). After teaching economics for seven years at the University of Michigan, he came to Columbia University in 1931 to his present position as professor of economics. During the years 1934-36 he directed a study of population redistribution through the Wharton School of the University of Pennsylvania. He was United States Labor Commissioner at Geneva, Switzerland, from 1936 to 1940, and has been the United States member of the governing body of the International Labor Office since 1936 and its chairman since 1939. He has been a delegate to numerous international labor conferences, and has written extensively on population and labor problems.

254

BIOGRAPHICAL NOTES

REINHOLD SCHAIRER

DR. SCHAIRER was born in Germany but became a voluntary exile from Nazism in 1933 and is now a British subject. His education included studies in law, education, philosophy, and sociology at the Universities of Tübingen, Geneva, and Berlin. During the first World War he was in Copenhagen as director of the Danish-German University Commission for the Education of Prisoners of War in Russia and also director of the Red Cross agency for the welfare of prisoners. During the time of the German Republic he founded and directed the Central Office of the German Universities for the Selection and Welfare of Gifted Students and the German Universities Office for Foreign Relations, was executive director of the German Universities Central Loan Bank and of the Scholarship Foundations of the German People, and was research director of the special commission of the German Republic on questions of youth unemployment. After leaving Germany when Hitler came to power, he became a lecturer in the Institute of Education of the University of London and head of its department for international studies and relations, and later served as a member of the British Committee on Educational Reconstruction. He came to the United States in 1940 on a Rockefeller scholarship to study American education, and now, beside being visiting professor of education in New York University, is director of research of the United States Committee on Educational Reconstruction.